Anonymus

Arts and Crafts Exhibition Society

Catalogue of the first Exhibition

Anonymus

Arts and Crafts Exhibition Society
Catalogue of the first Exhibition

ISBN/EAN: 9783742816764

Manufactured in Europe, USA, Canada, Australia, Japa

Cover: Foto ©Thomas Meinert / pixelio.de

Manufactured and distributed by brebook publishing software
(www.brebook.com)

Anonymus

Arts and Crafts Exhibition Society

ARTS & CRAFTS EXHIBITION SOCIETY

CATALOGVE OF THE FIRST EXHIBITION

THE NEW GALLERY
121 REGENT ST
1888

PREFACE.

THE decorative artist and the handicraftsman have hitherto had but little opportunity of displaying their work in the public eye, or rather of appealing to it upon strictly artistic grounds in the same sense as the pictorial artist ; and it is a somewhat singular state of things that at a time when the Arts are perhaps more looked after, and certainly more talked about, than they have ever been before, and the beautifying of houses, to those to whom it is possible, has become in some cases almost a religion, so little is known of the actual designer and maker (as distinct from

the proprietary manufacturer or middleman) of those familiar things which
contribute so much to the comfort
and refinement of life—of our chairs
and cabinets, our chintzes and wall-
papers, our lamps and pitchers—the
Lares and Penates of our households,
which with the touch of time and
association often come to be regarded
with so peculiar an affection.

Nor is this condition of affairs in
regard to applied Art without an explanation, since it is undeniable that
under the modern industrial system
that personal element, which is so
important in all forms of Art, has been
thrust further and further into the
background, until the production of
what are called ornamental objects,
and the supply of ornamental addi-
tions generally, instead of growing out
of organic necessities, have become,
under a misapplication of machinery,
driven by the keen competition of
trade, purely commercial affairs—
questions of the supply and demand
of the market artificially stimulated
and controlled by the arts of the ad-
vertiser and the salesman bidding
against each other for the favour of a
capricious and passing fashion which

too often takes the place of a real love of Art in our days.

Of late years, however, a kind of revival has been going on, as a protest against the conviction that, with all our modern mechanical achievements, comforts and luxuries, life is growing "uglier every day," as Mr. Morris puts it. Even our painters are driven to rely rather on the accidental beauty which, like a struggling ray through a London fog, sometimes illumes and transfigures the sordid commonplace of every day life. We cannot, however, live on sensational effects without impairing our sense of form and balance—of beauty, in short. We cannot concentrate our attention on pictorial and graphic art, and come to regard it as the one form worth pursuing, without losing our sense of construction and power of adaptation in design to all kinds of very different materials and purposes—that sense of relation — that architectonic sense which built up the great monuments of the past.

The true root and basis of all Art lies in the handicrafts. If there is no room or chance of recognition for really artistic power and feeling in design and craftsmanship—if Art is not recognized in the humblest object and material, and felt to be as valuable in its own way as the more highly rewarded pictorial skill—the arts cannot be in a sound condition ; and if artists cease to be found among the crafts there is great danger that they will vanish from the arts also, and become manufacturers and salesmen instead.

It is with the object of giving some visible expression to these views that the present Exhibition has been organized.

As was to be expected, many difficulties had to be encountered. In the endeavour to assign due credit to the responsible designer and workman, it has been sometimes difficult to do so amid the very numerous artificers who (in some cases) under our industrial conditions contribute to the production of a work.

The Committee of the Arts and Crafts Exhibition Society regret, too, that some leading firms in the supply of decorations have shown no disposition to exhibit under the condition that the names of the actual executants of any work shall be published.

At the same time, they would like to take the opportunity of thanking those who have come forward, together with all friends and supporters who have contributed to the Exhibition.

It will readily be understood that the organization of an exhibition of this character, and with such objects as we have in view, is a far less simple matter than a picture exhibition. Instead of having an array of artists whose names and addresses are in every catalogue, our constituency, as it were, outside the personal knowledge of the Committee, has had to be discovered. Under the designation of So-and-so and Co. many a skilful designer and craftsman may be concealed ; and individual and independent artists in design and handicraft are as yet few and far between.

However, in the belief, as elsewhere expressed, that it is little good nourishing the tree at the head if it is dying at the root, and that, living or dying, the desirability of an accurate diagnosis while there is any doubt of our artistic health will at once be admitted, the Society open their first Exhibition.

A series of papers upon various

Arts and Crafts follow, written by men
whose names, as will be observed, are
associated with the subjects of which
they treat, not only in the literary
sense, but as actual designers and
workmen.

WALTER CRANE.

Sept. 1888.

CONTENTS.

LECTURES.

The following Lectures, in connection with the Arts and Crafts Exhibition now open, will be given in the New Gallery, on Thursday evenings in November, at 8.30 p.m.

Thursday, Nov. 1.—"Tapestry and Carpet Weaving." William Morris.

Thursday, Nov. 8.—"Modelling and Sculpture." George Simonds.

Thursday, Nov. 15.—"Letterpress Printing." Emery Walker.

Thursday, Nov. 22.—"Bookbinding." T. J. Cobden-Sanderson.

Thursday, Nov. 29.—"Design" and Presidential Address. Walter Crane.

The object of the Lectures is two-fold: (1) to set out the aims of the Society, and (2), by demonstration and otherwise, to direct attention to the processes employed in the Arts and Crafts, and so to lay a foundation for a just appreciation both of the processes themselves and of their importance as methods of expression in design.

The Lectures will be given in the North Gallery, and after each Lecture all the galleries will be thrown open, and will remain open till 11 p m.

Admission by ticket. Price for a single lecture, 2s. 6d.; for the course, 10s.

For the admission of workers in any Art or Craft, tickets, to be filled in with the name, address, and Art or Craft of the worker, will be issued at 1s. each, or 25 for 20s., each entitling to admission to a single lecture.

Exhibitors, Artists, and Craftsmen mentioned in the Index to the Catalogue may have tickets free on application.

All tickets to be had at the Gallery.

Doors open at 8 p.m.; chair to be taken at 8.30 p.m.

Further information, if desired, to be had of the Hon. Lecture Secretary,

T. J. COBDEN-SANDERSON
Hendon N.W.

COMMITTEE.

HARRY BATES.
W. A. S. BENSON (*Hon. Treasurer*).
E. BURNE-JONES.
SOMERS CLARKE.
T. J. COBDEN-SANDERSON.
WALTER CRANE (*President*).
LEWIS F. DAY.
ONSLOW FORD.
F. GARRARD.
THOMAS GODFREY.
W. R. LETHABY.
HENRY LONGDEN.
W. H. LONSDALE.
MERVYN MACARTNEY.
WILLIAM DE MORGAN.
WILLIAM MORRIS.
J. HUNGERFORD POLLEN.
G. T. ROBINSON.
J. D. SEDDING.
HEYWOOD SUMNER.
EMERY WALKER.
THOMAS WARDLE.
METFORD WARNER.
STEPHEN WEBB.
N. H. J. WESTLAKE.

ERNEST RADFORD,
Secretary.

GUARANTORS.

C. W. MITCHELL, ESQ.
BUXTON MORRISH, ESQ.
MISS ORMEROD.
DR. PANKHURST.
MRS. PANKHURST.
J. F. PEARSON, ESQ.
A. RAFFALOVICH, ESQ.
REV. H. D. RAWNSLEY.
J. L. REDPATH, ESQ.
CHARLES RENSHAW, ESQ.
L. C. RIDDETT, ESQ.
GRAHAM ROBERTSON, ESQ.
MISS ROWE.
F. SCORER, ESQ.
MISS J. DURNING SMITH.
MISS M. A. SMITH.
R. SPENCER STANHOPE, ESQ.
J. E. TAYLOR, ESQ.
THE SKINNERS' COMPANY.
THE SOCIETY OF ARTS.
J. WILLIAM THOMPSON, ESQ.
C. TOMES, ESQ.
R. H. A. WILLIS, ESQ.
THE COMMITTEE.

INTRODUCTORY NOTES.

I. TEXTILES.

There are several ways of ornamenting a woven cloth : (1) real tapestry, (2) carpet weaving, (3) mechanical weaving, (4) printing or painting, and (5) embroidery. There has been no improvement (indeed, as to the main processes, no change) in the manufacture of the wares in all these branches since the fourteenth century, as far as the wares themselves are concerned ; whatever improvements have been introduced have been purely commercial, and have had to do merely with reducing the cost of production ; nay, more, the commercial improvements have on the whole been decidedly injurious to the quality of the wares themselves.

The noblest of the weaving arts is Tapestry, in which there is nothing mechanical : it may be looked upon as a mosaic of pieces of colour made up of dyed threads, and is capable of producing wall ornament of any degree of elaboration within the proper limits of duly considered decorative work.

As in all wall-decoration, the first thing to be considered in the designing of Tapestry is the force, purity, and elegance of the *silhouette* of the objects represented, and nothing vague or indeterminate is admissible. But special excellencies can be expected from it. Depth of tone, richness of colour, and exquisite gradation of tints are easily to be obtained in Tapestry; and it also demands that crispness and abundance of beautiful detail which was the especial characteristic of fully developed Mediæval Art. The style of even the best period of the Renaissance is wholly unfit for Tapestry : accordingly we find that Tapestry retained its Gothic character longer than any other of the pictorial arts. A comparison of the wall hangings in the Great Hall at Hampton Court with those in the Solar or drawing-room, will make this clear to any one not lacking in artistic perception : and the comparison is all the fairer, as both the Gothic tapestries of the Solar and the post-Gothic

hangings of the Hall are pre-eminently
good of their kinds.

Carpet-weaving is somewhat of the
nature of Tapestry : it also is wholly
unmechanical, but its use as a floor-
cloth somewhat degrades it, especially
in our northern or western countries,
where people come out of the muddy
streets into rooms without taking off
their shoes. Carpet-weaving un-
doubtedly arose among peoples living
a tent life, and for such a dwelling as
a tent carpets are the best possible
ornaments.

Carpets form a mosaic of small
squares of worsted, or hair, or silk
threads, tied into a coarse canvas,
which is made as the work progresses.
Owing to the comparative coarseness
of the work, the designs should always be very elementary in form, and
suggestive merely of forms of leafage,
flowers, beasts and birds, etc. The
soft gradations of tint to which Tapestry lends itself are unfit for Carpet-
weaving ; beauty and variety of colour
must be attained by harmonious
juxtaposition of tints, bounded by
judiciously chosen outlines ; and the
pattern should lie absolutely flat upon
the ground. On the whole, in design-

ing carpets the method of contrast is the best one to employ, and blue and red, quite frankly used, are the main colours on which the designer should depend.

In making the above remarks I have been thinking only of the genuine or hand-made carpets. The mechanically-made carpets of to-day must be looked upon as make-shifts for cheapness' sake. Of these, the velvet pile and Brussels are simply coarse worsted velvets woven over wires like other velvet, and cut, in the case of the velvet pile: and Kidderminster carpets are stout cloths, in which abundance of warp (a warp to each weft) is used for the sake of wear and tear. The velvet carpets need the same kind of design as to colour and quality as the real carpets, only as the colours are necessarily limited in number, and the pattern must repeat at certain distances, the design should be simpler and smaller than in a real carpet. A Kidderminster carpet calls for a small design in which the different planes, or plies, as they are called, are well interlocked.

Mechanical weaving has to repeat the pattern on the cloth within com-

paratively narrow limits ; the number
of colours also is limited in most cases
to four or five. In most cloths so
woven, therefore, the best plan seems
to be to choose a pleasant ground
colour, and to superimpose a pattern
mainly composed of either a lighter
shade of that colour, or a colour in no
very strong contrast to the ground ;
and then, if you are using several
colours, to light up this general arrangement either with a more forcible
outline, or by spots of stronger colour
carefully disposed. Often the lighter
shade on the darker suffices, and
hardly calls for anything else : some
very beautiful cloths are merely
damasks, in which the warp and weft
are of the same colour, but a different
tone is obtained by the figure and
the ground being woven with a longer
or shorter twill : the *tabby* being tied
by the warp very often, the *satin*
much more rarely. In any case, the
patterned webs produced by mechanical weaving, if the ornament is to be
effective and worth the doing, require
that same Gothic crispness and clearness of detail which has been spoken
of before : the geometrical structure
of the pattern, which is a necessity in

all recurring patterns, should be boldly
insisted upon, so as to draw the eye
from accidental figures, which the
recurrence of the pattern is apt to
produce.

The meaningless stripes and spots
and other tormentings of the simple
twill of the web, which are so common in the woven ornament of the
eighteenth century and in our own
times, should be carefully avoided :
all these things are the last resource
of a jaded invention and a contempt
of the simple and fresh beauty that
comes of a sympathetic *suggestion*
of natural forms : if the pattern be
vigorously and firmly drawn with a
true feeling for the beauty of line and
silhouette, the play of light and shade
on the material of the simple twill will
give all the necessary variety. I invite
my readers to make another comparison : to go to the South Kensington Museum and study the invaluable
fragments of the stuffs of the thirteenth
and fourteenth centuries of Syrian
and Sicilian manufacture, or the
almost equally beautiful webs of Persian design, which are later in date,
but instinct with the purest and best
Eastern feeling ; they may also note

the splendid stuffs produced mostly
in Italy in the later Middle Ages,
which are unsurpassed for richness
and *effect* of design, and when they
have impressed their minds with the
productions of this great historic
school, let them contrast with them
the work of the vile Pompadour
period, passing by the early seventeenth century as a period of transition
into corruption. They will then (if,
once more, they have real artistic
perception) see at once the difference
between the results of irrepressible
imagination and love of beauty, on the
one hand, and, on the other, of
restless and weary vacuity of mind,
forced by the exigencies of fashion to
do something or other to the innocent
surface of the cloth in order to distinguish it in the market from other
cloths ; between the handiwork of the
free craftsman doing as he *pleased*
with his work, and the drudgery of
the " operative " set to his task by the
tradesman competing for the custom
of a frivolous public, which had for-
gotten that there was such a thing
as art.

The next method of ornamenting
cloth is by painting it or printing on

it with dyes. As to the painting of
cloths with dyes by hand, which
is no doubt a very old and widely
practised art, it has now quite dis-
appeared; modern society not being
rich enough to pay the necessary
price for such work ; and its place has
now been taken by printing by block
or cylinder-machine. The remarks
made on the design for mechanically
woven cloths apply pretty much to
these printed stuffs : only in the first
place more play of delicate and pretty
colour is possible, and more variety of
colour also ; and in the second, much
more use can be made of hatching and
dotting, which are obviously suitable
to the method of block-printing. In
the many-coloured printed cloths
frank red and blue are again the
mainstays of the colour arrangement ;
these colours, softened by the paler
shades of red, outlined with black and
made more tender by the addition of
yellow in small quantities, mostly
forming part of brightish greens, make
up the colouring of the old Persian
prints, which carry the art as far as it
can be carried.

It must be added that no textile
ornament has suffered so much as

cloth-printing from those above-men-
tioned commercial inventions. A
hundred years ago the processes for
printing on cloth differed little from
those used by the Indians and Per-
sians ; and even up to within forty
years ago they produced colours that
were in themselves good enough, however inartistically they might be used.
Then came one of the most wonderful
and most useless of the inventions of
modern Chemistry, that of the dyes
made from coal-tar, producing a series
of hideous colours, crude, livid—and
cheap,—which every person of taste
loathes, but which nevertheless we can
by no means get rid of until we are
able to struggle successfully against
the doom of cheap and nasty which
has overtaken us.

Last of the methods of ornamenting
cloth comes Embroidery : of the design for which it must be said that one
of its aims should be the exhibition of
beautiful material. Furthermore, it is
not worth doing unless it is either
very copious and rich, or very delicate
—or both. For such an art nothing
patchy or scrappy, or half-starved,
should be done : there is no excuse
for doing anything which is not

strikingly beautiful ; and that more
especially as the exuberance of beauty
of the work of the East and of Mediæval Europe, and even of the time
of the Renaissance, is at hand to
reproach us. It may be well here to
warn those occupied in embroidery
against the feeble imitations of Japanese art which are so disastrously
common amongst us. The Japanese
are admirable naturalists, wonderfully
skilful draughtsmen, deft beyond all
others in mere execution of whatever
they take in hand ; and also great
masters of style within certain narrow
limitations. But with all this, a Japanese design is absolutely worthless
unless it is executed with Japanese
skill. In truth, with all their brilliant
qualities as handicraftsmen, which
have so dazzled us, the Japanese have
no architectural, and therefore no decorative, instinct. Their works of art
are isolated and blankly individual-
istic, and in consequence, unless where
they rise, as they sometimes do, to the
dignity of a suggestion for a picture
(always devoid of human interest),
they remain mere wonderful toys,
things quite outside the pale of the
evolution of art, which, I repeat,

cannot be carried on without the architectural sense that connects it with the history of mankind.

To conclude with some general remarks about designing for textiles : the aim should be to combine clearness of form and firmness of structure with the mystery which comes of abundance and richness of detail; and this is easier of attainment in woven goods than in flat painted decoration and paper-hangings ; because in the former the stuffs usually hang in folds and the pattern is broken more or less, while in the latter it is spread out flat against the wall. Do not introduce any lines or objects which cannot be explained by the structure of the pattern ; it is just this logical sequence of form, this growth which looks as if, under the circumstances, it could not have been otherwise, which prevents the eye wearying of the repetition of the pattern.

Never introduce any shading for the purpose of making an object look round ; whatever shading you use should be used for explanation only, to show what you mean by such and such a piece of drawing ; and even that you had better be sparing of.

Do not be afraid of large patterns; if properly designed they are more restful to the eye than small ones: on the whole, a pattern where the structure is large and the details much broken up is the most useful. Large patterns are not necessarily startling; this comes more of violent relief of the figure from the ground, or inharmonious colouring: beautiful and logical form relieved from the ground by well-managed contrast or gradation, and lying flat on the ground, will never weary the eye. Very small rooms, as well as very large ones, look best ornamented with large patterns, whatever you do with the middling-sized ones.

As final maxims: never forget the material you are working with, and try always to use it for doing what it can do best: if you feel yourself hampered by the material in which you are working, instead of being helped by it, you have so far not learned your business, any more than a would-be poet has, who complains of the hardship of writing in measure and rhyme. The special limitations of the material should be a pleasure to you, not a hindrance: a designer therefore should always thoroughly understand the processes of the special manufacture he is dealing with, or the result will be a mere *tour de force.* On the other hand, it is the pleasure in understanding the capabilities of a special material, and using them for suggesting (not imitating) natural beauty and incident, that gives the *raison d'être* of decorative art.

WILLIAM MORRIS.

II. OF DECORATIVE PAINTING AND DESIGN.

The term Decorative painting implies the existence of painting which is not decorative; a strange state of things for an art which primarily and pre-eminently appeals to the eye. If we look back to the times when the arts and crafts were in their most flourishing and vigorous condition, and dwelt together, like brethren, in unity—say to the fifteenth century —such a distinction did not exist. Painting only differed in its application, and in degree, not in kind. In the painting of a MS., of the panels of a coffer, of a ceiling, a wall, or an

altar-piece, the painter was alike—
however different his theme and conception—possessed with a paramount
impulse to decorate, to make the
space or surface he dealt with as
lovely to the eye in design and colour
as he had skill to do.

The art of painting has, however,
become considerably differentiated
since those days. We are here in
the nineteenth century encumbered
with many distinctions in the art.
There is obviously much painting
which is not decorative, or ornamental
in any sense, which has indeed quite
other objects. It may be the presentment of the more superficial
natural facts, phases, or accidents of
light ; the pictorial dramatizing of
life or past history ; the pointing of a
moral ; or the embodiment of romance
and poetic thought or symbol. Not but
what it is quite possible for a painter
to deal with such things and yet to
produce a work that shall be decorative.

A picture, of course, may be a piece
of decorative art of the most beautiful
kind, but to begin with, if it is an
easel picture, it is not necessarily
related to anything but itself: its

painter is not bound to consider anything outside its own dimensions ;
and, indeed, the practice of holding
large and mixed picture-shows has
taught him the uselessness of so
doing.

Then too, the demand for literal
presentment of the superficial facts or
phases of nature often removes the
painter and his picture still further
from the architectural, decorative, and
constructive artist and the handicraftsman, who are bound to think of
plan, and design, and materials—of the
adaptation of their work, in short—
while the painter seeks only to be an
unbiased recorder of all accidents and
sensational conditions of nature and
life. And so we get our illustrated
newspapers on a grand scale.

An illustrated newspaper, however,
in spite of the skill and enterprise it
may absorb, is not somehow a joy for
ever ; and, after all, if literalism and
instantaneous appearances are the
only things worth striving for in painting, the photograph beats any painter
at that.

If truth is the object of the modern
painter of pictures—truth as distinct
from or opposed to beauty—beauty is

certainly the object of the decorative
painter, but beauty not necessarily
severed from truth.   Without beauty,
however, decoration has no reason for
existence, indeed it can hardly be
said to exist.

Next to beauty, the first essential
of a decoration is that it shall be related to its environment, that it shall
express or acknowledge the conditions under which it exists.   If a
fresco on a wall, for instance, it adorns
the wall without attempting to look
like a hole cut in it through which
something is accidentally seen ; if a
painting on a vase, it acknowledges
the convexity of the shape, and helps
to express instead of contradicting it ;
if on a panel in a cabinet or door, it
spreads itself in an appropriate filling
on an organic plan to cover it ; being,
in short, ornamental by its very
nature, its first business is to ornament.

There exist, therefore, certain de-
finite tests for the work of the decorative artist.   Does the design fit its
place and material ?   Is it in scale
with its surroundings and in harmony
with itself ?   Is it fair and lovely in
colour ?   Has it beauty and invention ?

Has it thought and poetic feeling?
These are the demands a decorator
has to answer, and by his answer he
must stand or fall; but such questions show that the scope of decoration is no mean one.

It must be acknowledged that a
mixed exhibition does not easily
afford the fairest or completest tests
of such qualities. An exhibition is
at best a compromise, a convenience,
a means of comparison, and to en-
able work to be shown to the public;
but of course work is, after all, only
really and properly exhibited when it
is in the place and position and light
for which it was destined. The tests
by which to judge a designer's work
are only complete then.

As are the stem and branches to the
leaves, flowers, and fruit of a tree, so
is design to painting. In decoration
one cannot exist without the other,
as the beauty of a figure depends
upon the well-built and proportioned
skeleton and its mechanism. You cannot separate a house from its plan and
foundations. So it is in decoration;
often thought of lightly as something
trivial and superficial, a merely aim-
less combination of curves and colours,

or a mere réchauffé of the dead languages of art, but really demanding the best thought and capacity of a man ; and in the range of its application it is not less comprehensive.

The mural painter is not only a painter, but a poet, historian, dramatist, philosopher. What should we know, how much should we realize, of the ancient world and its life without him, and his brother the architectural sculptor? How would ancient Egypt live without her wall paintings—or Rome, or Pompeii, or Mediæval Italy? How much beauty as well as of history is contained in the illuminated pages of the books of the Middle Ages!

Some modern essays in mural painting show that the habit of mind and method of work fostered by the production of trifles for the picture market are not favourable to monumental painting. Neither the mood nor the skill, indeed, can be grown like a mushroom ; such works as the Sistine Chapel, the Stanzi of Raphael, or the Apartimenti Borgia, are the result of long practice through many centuries, and intimate relationship and harmony in the arts, as well as a certain unity of public sentiment.

The true soil for the growth of the painter in this higher sense is a rich and varied external life; familiarity from early youth with the uses of materials and methods, and the hand facility which comes of close and constant acquaintanceship with the tools of the artist, who sums up and includes in himself other crafts, such as modelling, carving, and the hammering of metal, architectural design, and a knowledge of all the ways man has used to beautify and deck the surroundings and accessories of life to satisfy his delight in beauty.

We know that painting was strictly an applied art in its earlier history, and all through the Middle Ages painters were in close alliance with the other crafts of design, and their work in one craft no doubt re-acted on and influenced that in another, while each was kept distinct. At all events painters like Albert Dürer and Holbein were also masters of design in all ways.

Through the various arts and crafts of the Greek, Mediæval, or Early Renaissance periods, there is evident, from the examples which have come down to us, a certain unity and com-

mon character in design : and yet,
asserting itself through all diverse in-
dividualities, each art is kept distinct,
with a complete recognition of the
capacity and advantages of its own
particular method and purpose.

In our own age for various rea-
sons (social, commercial, economic),
the specialized and purely pictorial
painter is dominant. His aims and
methods influence other arts and crafts,
but by no means advantageously as a
rule ; since, unchecked by judicious
ideas of design, attempts are made in
unsuitable materials to produce so-
called realistic force and superficial
and accidental appearances, dependent
on peculiar qualities of lighting and
atmosphere, quite out of place in any
other method than painting, or in any
place but an easel picture.

From such tendencies, such in-
fluences as these, in the matter of
applied art and design, we are striving
to recover. One of the first results is,
perhaps, this apparently artificial distinction between decorative and other
painting. But along with this we
have painters whose easel pictures are
in feeling and treatment quite adapt-
able as wall and panel decorations,

and they are painters who, as a rule, have studied other methods in art, and drawn their inspiration from the mode of Mediæval or Early Renaissance times.

Much might be said of different methods and materials of work in decorative painting, but I have hardly space here. The decorative painter prefers a certain flatness of effect, and therefore such methods as fresco, in which the colours are laid on while the plaster ground is wet, and tempera naturally appeal to him. In the latter the colours ground in water and used with size, or white and yolk of egg, or prepared with starch, worked on a dry ground, drying lighter than when they are put on, have a peculiar luminous quality, while the surface is free from any gloss. Both these methods need direct painting and finishing as the work proceeds.

By a method of working in ordinary oil colours on a ground of fibrous plaster, using rectified spirit of turpentine or benzine as a medium, much of the quality of fresco or tempera may be obtained, with the advantage that the plaster ground may be a moveable panel.

There are, however, other fields for
the decorative painter than wall painting ; as, for instance, domestic furniture, which may vary in degree of
elaboration from the highly ornate
cassone or marriage coffer of Mediæval Italy to the wreaths and sprays
which decked chairs and bed-posts
even within our century. There has
been of late some revival of decorative painting as applied chiefly to the
panels of cabinets, or to piano fronts
and cases.

The same causes produce the same
results. With the search after, and
desire for, beauty in life, we are again
driven to study the laws of beauty
in design and painting; and in so
doing painters will find again the
lost thread, the golden link of connection and intimate association with
the sister arts and handicrafts, where-
of none is before or after another, none
is greater or less than the other.

WALTER CRANE.

III. OF WALL PAPERS.

While the tradition and practice of mural painting as applied to interior walls and ceilings of houses still lingers in Italy, in the form of often skilful if not always tasteful tempera work, in more western countries, like England, France, and America, under the economic conditions and customs of commercial civilization, with its smoky cities, and its houses built by the hundred to one pattern, perhaps, and let on short terms, mural painting as regards domestic decoration—except in the case of a few wealthy freeholders—has ceased to exist. Its place has been taken by what after all is but a substitute for it, namely, wall paper.

I am not aware that any specimen of wall paper has been discovered that has claims to any higher antiquity than the sixteenth century, and it only came much into use in the last, increasing in the present, until it has become well nigh a universal covering for domestic walls, and at the same time has shown a remarkable development in design, varying from very unpretending patterns, and printings in one colour, to elaborate block-printed designs in many colours, besides cheap machine-printed papers, where all the tints in the design are printed from rollers at one operation.

Since Mr. William Morris has shown what beauty and character in pattern, and good and delicate choice of tint can do for us, giving in short a new impulse in design, a great amount of ingenuity and enterprise has been spent on wall papers in England, and in the better kinds a very distinct advance has been made upon the patterns of inconceivable hideousness, often of French origin, of the period of the Second Empire—a period which perhaps represents the most degraded level of taste in decoration generally.

The designer of patterns for wall papers heretofore has been content to imitate other materials, and adapt the characteristics of the patterns found, say, in silk damask hangings or tapestry, or even imitate the veining of wood, or marble, or tiles ; but with the revival of interest in art, the study of its history, and knowledge of style, a new impulse has been

given, and patterns are constructed
with more direct reference to their
beauty, and interest as such, while
strictly adapted to the methods of
manufacture. Great pains are often
taken by our principal makers to
secure good designs and harmonious
colourings, and though a manufacturer
and director of works is always more
or less controlled by the exigencies
of the market and the demands of
the tentative salesman — considerations which have no natural connection with art, though highly important as economic conditions affect-
ing its welfare — very remarkable
results have been produced, and a
special development of applied design
may almost be said to have come into
existence with the modern use of wall
papers. The manufacture suffers like
most others from the keenness and
unscrupulousness of commercial competition, which leads to the production
of specious imitations of *bonâ fide*
designs, and to the unauthorized use
of designs originally intended for
other purposes. This of course presses
unfairly upon the more conscientious
maker, so long as the public do not
decline to be deceived.

English wall papers are made in
lengths 21 inches wide. French wall
papers are 18 inches wide. It is obvious to any one who has seen the
printers at work that a wider block
than 21 inches would be unwieldy,
since the block is manipulated by
hand, being suspended from above by
a cord, and guided by the workman's
hand from the "sieve," a piece of
felt covered with colour, on which it
is dipped, to the paper flat on a table
before him.

The designer must work to the
given width, and though his design
may vary in depth, must never exceed
21 inches square, except where double
blocks are used, as is sometimes the
case with the more costly kind of wall
papers. (For examples see Catalogue,
Nos. 69, 224, 225.) His main business
is to devise his pattern so that it will
repeat satisfactorily over an indefinite
wall space without running into awk-
ward holes or lines. It may be easy
enough to draw a spray or two of
leaves or flowers which will stand by
themselves, but to combine them in
an organic pattern which shall repeat
pleasantly over a wall surface requires
much ingenuity and a knowledge of

the conditions of the manufacture, apart from play of fancy and artistic skill.

One way of concealing the joints of the repeat of the pattern is by contriving what is called a drop-repeat, so that, in hanging, the paper-hanger, instead of placing each repeat of pattern side by side, is enabled to join the pattern at a point its own depth below, which varies the effect, and arranges the chief features or masses on an alternating plan.

The modern habit of regarding the walls of a room chiefly as a background to pictures, furniture, or people, and, perhaps, the smallness of the average room, have brought rather small, thickly dispersed leafy patterns into vogue, retiring in colour for the most part. Where, however, we used to see rotund and accidental bunches of roses (the pictorial or sketchy treatment of which contrasted awkwardly with their formal repetition), we now get a certain sense of adaptation, and the necessity of a certain flatness of treatment ; and most of us who have given much thought to the subject feel that when natural forms are dealt with, under such conditions, sugges-

tion is better than any attempt at
realization, or naturalistic or pictorial
treatment, and that a design must be
constructed upon some systematic
plan, if not absolutely controlled by a
geometric basis.

Wall papers are printed from blocks
usually cut in pear-tree wood, but for
fine outlines and other delicate work
flat brass wire driven edgeways into
the wood block is used. One block
for each tint is generally used. First
one colour is printed on a length of
paper, a piece of 12 yards long and
21 inches wide, which is passed over
sticks suspended across the workshop.
When the first colour is dry the next
is printed, and so on—the colours being mixed with size and spread on felt
in shallow trays or wells, into which
the blocks are dipped. But at times,
by processes called "blending" and
"patching," several tints are printed
together by one block. An example
of this kind of printing is to be seen
in the exhibit numbered 96 in the
Catalogue, in which eight colours are
laid at one time.

A cheaper kind is printed by steam
power from rollers on which the design has been reproduced in the same

way by brass wire, which holds the colour; but in the case of machine-printed papers all the tints are printed at once. Thus the pattern is often imperfect and blurred.

A more elaborate and costly kind of wall paper is the stamped and gilded kind, in emulation of stamped and gilded leather, which it resembles in effect and quality of surface. For this method the design is reproduced in relief as a repoussé brass plate, and from this a mould or matrix is made, and the paper being damped, is stamped in a press into the matrix, and so takes the pattern in relief, which is covered generally with white metal and lacquered to a gold hue, and this again may be rubbed in with black, which by filling the interstices gives emphasis to the design and darkens the gold to bronze; or the gilded surface may be treated in any variety of colour by means of painting or lacquer, or simply relieved by colouring the ground.

Few of us, however, own our own walls, or the ground they stand upon: few of us can afford to employ ourselves or skilled artists and craftsmen in painting our rooms with beautiful

fancies : but if we can get well designed repeating patterns by the yard,
in agreeable tints, with a pleasant
flavour perchance of nature or antiquity, for a few shillings or pounds,
ought we not to be happy ?   At all
events wall paper makers should
naturally think so.

WALTER CRANE.

IV. FICTILES.

Earliest amongst the inventions of
man and his endeavours to unite Art
with Craft is the Fictile Art. His first
needs in domestic life, his first utensils, his first efforts at civilization,
came from the Mother Earth, whose
son he believed himself to be, and his
ashes or his bones returned to Earth
enshrined in the fictile vases he created
from their common clay. And these
Fictiles tell the story of his first Art-
instincts, and of his yearnings to unite
beauty with use. They tell, too, more
of his history than any other art has
enshrined and preserved, for almost
all we know of many a people and
many a tongue is learned from the
fictile record, the sole relic of past

civilizations which the Destroyer Time has left us.

Begun in the simplest fashion, fashioned by the simplest means, created from the commonest materials, Fictile Art grew with man's intellectual growth, and Fictile Craft grew with his knowledge, the latter conquering, in this our day, when the craftsman strangles the artist alike in this as in all other arts. To truly foster and forward the art the craftsman and the artist should, where possible, be united, or at least should work in common, as was the case when, in each civilization, the Potter's Art flourished most, and when the scientific base was of less account than was the art employed upon it. In its earliest stages the local clay sufficed for the formative portion of the work, and the faiences of most European countries offer more artistic results to us than do the more scientifically compounded porcelains. In the former case the native clay seemed more easily to ally itself with native art, to record more of current history, to create artistic genius rather than to be content with attempting to copy misunderstood efforts of other peoples and other times. But when science ransacked the earth for foreign bodies and ingredients, foreign decorative ideas came with them and Fictile Art was no more a vernacular one. It attempted to disguise itself, to show the craftsman superior to the artist ; and then came the Manufacturer and the reign of quantity over quality, the casting in moulds by the gross and the printing by the thousands. Be it understood these remarks only apply to the introduction of porcelain into Europe. In the East, where the clay is native, the art is native ; the potter's hand and the wheel yet maintain the power of giving the potter his individuality as the creator and the artist, and save him from being but the servant and the slave of a machine.

Between faience and porcelain comes, midway, Stoneware, in which many wonderfully, and some fearfully, made things have been done of late, but which possess the combined qualities of faience and porcelain,—the ease of manipulation of the former, and the hardness and durability of the latter ; but the tendency to over elaborate the detail of its decoration, and rely less on the beauty of its semi-

glossy surface than on meretricious
ornament, has rather spoiled a very
hopeful movement in ceramic art.
Probably the wisest course to pursue
at the present would be to pay more
attention to faiences decorated with
simple glazes or with "slip" decoration, and this especially in modelled
work. A continuation of the artistic
career of the Della Robbia family
is yet an unfulfilled desideratum notwithstanding that glazed faiences
have never since their time ceased to
be made, and that glazed figure work
of large scale prevailed in the
eighteenth century. Unglazed terra
cotta, an artistic product eminently
suited to our climate and to our urban
architecture, has but partially developed itself, and this more in the
direction of moulded and cast work
than that of really plastic art ; and al-
beit that from its dawn to this present
the fictile art has been exercised abun-
dantly, its rôle is by no means ex-
hausted. The artist and the craftsman
have yet a wide field before them, but
it would be well that the former should,
for some while to come, take the lead.
Science has too long reigned supreme
in a domain wherein she should have

been not more than equal sovereign. She has had her triumphs, great triumphs too, triumphs which have been fraught with good in an utilitarian sense, but she has tyrannized too rigidly over the realm of Art. Let us now try to equalize the dual rule.

G. T. ROBINSON.

V. METAL WORK.

In discussing the artistic aspect of metal work, we have to take into account the physical properties and appropriate treatment of the following metals: the precious metals, gold and silver; copper, both pure and alloyed with other metals, especially tin and zinc in various proportions to form the many kinds of brass and bronze; lead, with a group of alloys of which pewter is typical; and iron, in the three forms of cast iron, wrought iron, and steel. All these have been made to serve the purpose of the artist, and the manipulation of them, while presenting many differences in detail, presents certain broad characteristics in common which distinguish them from the raw material of other crafts. Whether they are found native in the metallic state as is usual in the case of gold, or combined with many other minerals in the form of ore as is more common with other metals, fire is the primal agency by which they are made available for our needs. The first stage in their manipulation is to melt and cast them into ingots of a size convenient to the purpose intended. Secondly, all these metals when pure, and many alloys, are in varying degree malleable and ductile, are in fact, if sufficient force be applied, plastic. Hence arises the first broad division in the treatment of metals. The fluid metal may, by the use of suitable moulds, be cast at once to the shape required, or the casting may be treated merely as the starting-point for a whole series of operations—forging, rolling, chipping, chasing, wiredrawing, and many more. Another property of the metals which must be noticed is, that not only can separate masses of metals be melted down and fused into one, but it is possible, under various conditions, of which the one invariably necessary is perfectly clean surfaces of contact, to unite separate portions of the same or different metals without fusion of the mass. For our present purpose the most important instance of this is the process of soldering, by which two surfaces are united by the application of sufficient heat to melt more fusible metal which is introduced between them, and which combines with both so as firmly to unite them on solidifying. Closely allied to this are the processes by which one metal is, for purposes of adornment or preservation from corrosion, coated with a thin film or deposit of another, usually more costly, metal.

Though hereafter electro-metallurgy may assert its claim to artistic originality as a third division, for the present all metal work, so far as its artistic aspect depends upon process, falls naturally into one of the two broad divisions of cast metal and wrought metal. Both have been employed from a time long anterior to written history; ornaments of beaten gold, and tools of cast bronze, are alike found among the relics of very early stages of civilization, and in early stages both alike are artistic. The choice between the two processes is determined by such considerations as convenience of manufacture and the physical properties of the metals, and the different purposes in view. When a thick and comparatively massive shape is required, it is often easier to cast it at once. For thinner and lighter forms it is usually more convenient to treat the ingot or crude product of the furnace as mere raw material for a long series of workings under the hammer, or its patent mechanical equivalents, the rolling and pressing mills of modern mechanics. The choice is further influenced by the toughness generally characteristic of wrought metal, whereas the alloys which yield the cleanest castings are by no means universally the best in other respects. Iron is the extreme instance of this : ordinary cast iron, an impure form of the metal, is too brittle to be worked under the hammer, but is readily cast into moulds, being fluid at a temperature which, though high, is easily obtained in a blast furnace. Wrought iron, however, which is usually obtained from cast iron by a process called puddling, whereby the impurities are burnt out, does not, at a like temperature, become fluid enough to pour into moulds ; but, on the other hand, pieces at a white heat can be united into a solid mass by skilful hammering, a process which, from the further fact that from its great hardness iron is usually worked hot under the hammer, is specially distinctive of the blacksmith's craft. In no other metal is the separation between the two branches of cast and wrought so wide as in iron. The misdirected skill, moreover, of some modern iron-founders has caused the name of cast iron to be regarded as the very negative of art, and has even thrown suspicion on the process of casting itself as one of questionable honesty. Nevertheless, as a craft capable of giving final shape to metal, casting has manifestly an artistic aspect, and, in fact, bronze statuary, a fine art pure and simple, is reproduced from the clay model merely by moulding and casting. We must therefore look for the artistic conditions of casting in the preparation of the model or pattern, the impress of which in sand or loam forms the mould ; the pattern may be carved in wood or modelled in clay, but the handling of the wood or clay is modified by the conditions

under which the form is reproduced.
And lastly, the finished object may
either retain the surface formed as
the metal solidifies, as in the case of
the bronzes cast by the wax process,
or the skin may be removed by the
use of cutting tools, chisels and files
and gravers, so that, as in the case of
many of the better French bronzes,
the finished work is strictly carved
work. On the contrary, much silver-
smith's work, as well as such simple
objects as Chinese gongs and Indian
" lotahs," after being cast approxi-
mately to shape, are finished by hammer work, that is, treated as plastic
material with tools that force the
material into shape instead of cutting
the shape out of the mass by remov-
ing exterior portions of material. Attempts to imitate both processes by
casting only, thus dispensing with the
cost of finishing, are common, but as
they dispense likewise with all beauty
in the product, even if they do not
substitute varnished and tinted zinc
for better metal, their success is commercial only.

We have thus three characteristic
kinds of surface resulting from the
conditions of treatment, marking out

three natural divisions of the art (and
be it noted that questions of surface
or texture are all important in the
arts; beauty is skin deep).   First, the
natural skin of the metal solidified in
contact with the mould, and more or
less closely imitative of the surface of
the original model, usually for our
purposes a plastic surface; secondly,
there is carved, technically called
chased work; and thirdly, beaten or
wrought work, which in ornament is
termed embossing.

Superimposed on these we have the
cross divisions of the crafts according
to the special metal operated on, and
in the existing industrial organization
the groups thus obtained have to be
further divided into many sub-heads,
according to the articles produced;
and finally another commercial distinction has to be drawn which greatly
affects the present condition of handicraft, that is, the division of the several
trades into craftsmen and salesmen.
There can be no doubt that the extent
of the existing dissociation of the producing craftsman from the consumer
is an evil for the arts, and that the
growing preponderance of great stores
is inimical to excellence of workman-

ship. It is, perhaps, an advantage for the workmen to be relieved from the office of salesman ; the position of the village smith plying his calling in face of his customers might not suit every craft, but the services of the middleman are dearly bought at the price of artistic freedom. It is too often in the power of the middleman to dictate the quality of workmanship, too often his seeming interest to ordain that it shall be bad.

The choice of a metal for any particular purpose is determined by physical properties combined with considerations of cost. Iron, if only for its cheapness, is the material of the largest works of metal; while in the form of steel it is the best available material for many very small works, watch-springs for instance : it has the defect of liability to rust ; the surfaces of other metals may tarnish, but iron rusts through. For the present only one application of cast iron concerns us — its use for grates and stoves. The point to remember is, that as the material has but little beauty, its employment should be restricted to the quantity prescribed by the demands of utility. Wrought iron, on

the contrary, gives very great scope
to the artist, and it offers this peculiar advantage, that the necessity of
striking while the iron is hot enforces
such free dexterity of handling in the
ordinary smith, that he has comparatively little to learn if set to produce
ornamental work, and thus renewed
interest in the art has found craftsmen enough who could readily re-
spond to the demand made upon
them.

Copper, distinguished among metals
by its glowing red tint, has as a material for artistic work been over-
shadowed by its alloys, brass and
bronze ; partly because they make
sounder castings, partly, it is to be
feared, from the approach of their
colour to gold. Holding an intermediate position between iron and the
precious metals, they are the material
of innumerable household utensils and
smaller architectural fittings.

Lead, tin, and zinc, scarcely con-
cern the artist to-day, though neither
plumber nor pewterer has always
been restricted to plain utilitarian-
ism. Gold and silver have been
distinguished in all ages as the precious metals, both for their compara-

tive rarity and their freedom from
corrosion, and their extreme beauty.
They are both extremely malleable
and very readily worked. Unhappily
there is little original English work
being done in these metals. The more
ordinary wares have all life and feeling taken out of them by mechanical
finish, an abrasive process being employed to remove every sign of tool-
marks. The all important surface is
thus obliterated. As to design, fashion
oscillates between copies of one past
period and another. A comparison
of one of these copies with an original
will make the distinction between the
work of a man paid to do his quickest
and one paid to do his best clearer
than volumes of description. Indeed,
when all is said, a writer can but indi-
cate the logic that underlies the craft,
or hint at the relation which subsists
between the process, the material,
and the finished ware: the distinction
between good and bad in art eludes
definition; it is not an affair of
reason, but of perception.

W. A. S. BENSON.

VI. STONE AND WOOD CARVING.

The crafts of the stone and wood carver may fairly be taken in review at the same time, although they differ in themselves.

In these days the " sculptor " is far too often a man who would think it a condescension to execute decorative work. From his method of training he has, in fact, lost all knowledge how to produce such work. He understands nothing of design in a wide sense, and being able to model a figure with tolerable success, rests therewith content. The result is, that his work is wanting in sympathy with its surroundings ; it does not fall into its place as part of a complete conception.

It was not so when sculpture and what, for want of a better term, we have called "stone and wood carving" were at their prime.

The Greek craftsman could produce both the great figure of the God which stood alone as the central object in the temple, and (working in sympathy

with the architect) the decorative
sculpture of less importance which
stood around, and without which the
beauty of the fabric was incomplete.

So also the Florentines did not
think themselves degraded by working
at a door, a tomb, with its complete
surroundings, the enclosure of a choir,
etc.

In the great days of Mediæval
Architecture sculpture played a part
of equal importance, and the works
then produced are not only excellent
in themselves, but are thoroughly a
part of the building they adorn. How
thoroughly unfinished would the west
front of the Cathedral at Wells or the
portals of the Cathedrals of Amiens
and Reims be without their sculpture.

How rarely can we say this of work
similarly applied in our modern buildings. The figures are " stood about "
like ornaments on the mantel-piece.
The architect seems as unable to prepare for them as the sculptor to produce them. We seldom see congruity
even between the figure and the
pedestal on which it stands.

The want of this extended sympathy leads to another ill result.
Wood, stone, and metal, different as

they are, are handled by the craftsman in much the same fashion.

The model in clay seems to stand
behind everything. The "artist" pro-
duces the model, and the subordinates
must work it out in one or another
material.

The natural limitations fixed by
the different qualities of the materials
have not been taken into consideration from the moment the design was
first conceived. Marble, stones, some
hard, some soft, terra cotta, metals or
wood, each demands a difference of
treatment. The fibrous nature of
wood enables the craftsman to produce work which would fall to pieces
at the first blow if executed in stone.
The polished and varied surface of
marble demands a treatment of surface and section of mouldings which
in stone would seem tame and poor.
Again, we must not forget that large
works in marbles and stones are built
up. They are composed of many
blocks standing one on the other.
With wood it is quite different. Used
in thick pieces it splits : good wood-
work is framed together, the framing
and intermediate panelling lending itself to the richest decoration ; but

anything in the design which suggests
stone construction is obviously wrong.
In short, wood is fibrous and tena-
cious, and in planks or slabs ; stone
or marble is of close, even texture, and
brittle, and in blocks.

The tools and methods of handling
them used by the wood carver differ
in many respects from those used by
the stone or marble worker. One
material is scooped and cut out, the
other is attacked by a constant repetition of blows, the instrument used
being impelled by a mallet.

In the history of Mediæval Art we
find that the craft of the stone carver
was perfectly understood long before
that of his brother craftsman in wood.
Whilst the first had all through
Europe attained great perfection in
the thirteenth century, the second
did not reach the same standard till
the fifteenth, and with the classic revival it died out. Nothing displays
more fully the adaptation of design
and decoration to the material than
much of the fifteenth century stall
work in our English cathedrals. These
could only be executed in wood ; the
design is suited to that material only ;
but when the Italian influence creeps

in the designs adopted are in fact suited to fine stone, marble, or alabaster, and not to wood.

Until the craftsman in stone and wood is more of an architect, and the architect more of a craftsman, we cannot hope for improvement.

SOMERS CLARKE.

VII. FURNITURE.

The institution of schools of art and design, and the efforts of serials and magazines devoted to artistic matters, have had their proper effect in the creation of a pretty general distaste for the clumsy and inartistic forms which characterized cabinets and furniture generally some years back. Unfortunately for the movement, some manufacturers saw in the demand thus created for better and more artistic shapes their opportunity to produce bad and ill-made copies of good designs, copies which undermined the self-respect of the unfortunate man (frequently a good and sufficient craftsman) whose ill hap it was to be

obliged to make them, and vexed
the soul of the equally unfortunate
purchaser.

The introduction of **machinery** for
moulding, which left only the fitting
and polishing to be done by **the**
craftsman, and which enabled manufacturers to produce two or three
cabinets in the time formerly occupied
in the making of one, was all against
the quality and stability of the work.
No good work was ever done in a
hurry : the craftsman may be rapid,
but his rapidity is the result of very
deliberate thought, and not of hurry.
Good furniture, however, cannot be
made rapidly. All wood, no matter
how long it is kept, nor how dry it
may be superficially, will always shrink
again when cut into.

It follows that the longer the in-
terval between the cutting up of the
wood, and its fitting together, the
better for the work. In the old times
the parts of a cabinet lay about in the
workman's benchway for weeks, and
even months, and were continually
turned over and handled by him while
he was engaged on the mouldings and
other details. The wood thus became
really dry, and no further shrinkage

could take place after it was put
together.

A word here about the designing of
cabinets.

Modern furniture designers are far
too much influenced by considerations
of style, and sacrifice a good deal that
is valuable in order to conform to
certain rules which, though sound
enough in their relation to architecture,
do not really apply to furniture at all.
Much more pleasing, and not necessarily less artistic work would be
produced, were designers, and handicraftsmen too, encouraged to allow
their imagination more scope, and to
get more of their own individuality
into their work, instead of being the
slaves of styles invented by people
who lived under quite different conditions to those now prevailing.

Mouldings as applied to cabinets are
nearly always too coarse, and project
too much. This applies equally to
the carvings, which should always be
quite subordinate to the general design and mouldings, and (in its application to surfaces) should be in low
relief. This is quite compatible with
all necessary vigour as well as refinement. The idea that boldness—viz.,

high projection of parts in carving—
has anything to do with vigour is a
common one, but is quite erroneous.
All the power and vigour which he is
capable of putting into anything, the
clever carver can put into a piece of
ornament which shall not project more
than a quarter of an inch from the
ground in any part. Indeed, I have
known good carvers who did their
best work within those limits. Knowledge of line, of the management of
planes, and dexterity in the handling
of surfaces, are all that he requires.
Another common mistake is to suppose that smoothness of surface has
anything to do with finish properly
so called. If only half the time which
is commonly spent in smoothing and
polishing carved surfaces was devoted
to the more thorough study and development of the various parts of the
design, and the correction of the outlines, the surface might very well be
left to take care of itself, and the work
would be the better for it.

There is not space in this paper to
do more than glance at a few other
methods in ordinary use for cabinet
decoration. Marquetry, inlays of
ivory and various other materials,

has always been extensively used,
and sometimes with excellent effect.
In many old examples the surface of
the solid wood was cut away to the
pattern, and various other kinds of
wood pressed into the lines so sunk.
The method more generally adopted
now is to insert the pattern into
veneer which has been prepared to
receive it, and mount the whole on a
solid panel or shape with glue.

The besetting sin of the modern
designer or maker of marquetry is a
tendency to "loud" colour and violent
contrasts of both colour and grain.
It is common to see as many as a
dozen different kinds of wood used in
the decoration of a modern cabinet—
some of them stained woods, and the
colours of no two of them in harmony.

The best work in this kind depends for its effect on a rich, though
it may be low tone of colour. It
is seldom that more than two or
three different kinds of wood are used,
but each kind is so carefully selected
for the purpose of the design, and is
used in so many different ways, that,
while the all important "tone" is kept
throughout, the variety of surface is
almost infinite. For this reason,

though it is not necessary that the designer should actually cut the work himself, it is most essential that he should always be within call of the cutter, and should himself select every piece of wood which is introduced into the design. This kind of work is sometimes shaded with hot sand ; at other times a darker wood is introduced into the pattern for the shadows. The latter is the better way ; the former is the cheaper.

As to the polishing of cabinet work, I have so strong an objection in this connection to the French polisher and all his works and ways, that, notwithstanding the popular prejudice in favour of brilliant surfaces, I would have none of him. Formerly the cabinet - maker was accustomed to polish his own work, sometimes by exposing the finished surfaces to the light for a few weeks in order to darken them, and then applying beeswax with plentiful rubbing. This was the earliest and the best method, but in later times a polish composed of naphtha and shellac was used. The latter polish, though open to many of the objections which may be urged against that now in use, was at least

hard and lasting, which can hardly
be said of its modern substitute.

The action of the more reputable
cabinet-making firms has been, of late,
almost wholly in the direction of
better design and construction ; but a
still better guarantee of progress in
the future of the craft is found in the
fact that the craftsman who takes an
artistic and intelligent, and not a
merely mechanical interest in his
work, is now often to be met with.
To such men greater individual freedom is alone wanting.

STEPHEN WEBB.

VIII. STAINED GLASS.

In a collection of works such as
those now brought together, a specimen of stained glass must not be judged
from the standpoint of the mere ar-
chæologist. The art had languished
during the seventeenth and eighteenth
centuries, and began to lift its head
only with the revived study of the architecture of the Middle Ages. To
attain archæological correctness was
one of the chief aims of the revivalists,

The crude draughtsmanship of the ancient craftsman was imitated, but the result lacked the spirit and charm of the original. Under such conditions the modern worker in stained glass produced things possibly more hideous than the world ever saw before.

Departing altogether from the traditions of the Mediæval school, there has arisen another school which has found its chief exponents at Munich, and has produced transparencies no better than painted blinds.

What, then, it may be asked, are the limiting conditions, imposed upon him by the nature of the material, within which the craftsman must work to produce a satisfactory result?

In the first place, a stained window is not an easel picture. It does not stand within a frame, it is not an object to be looked at by itself, but must play its part in the adornment of the building in which it is placed, being subordinated to the effect the interior is intended to produce as a whole. It is, in fact, but one of many parts that go to *produce a complete result.* A visit to one of our mediæval churches, such as York Minster, Gloucester Cathe-

dral, or Malvern Priory Church, each
of which retains much of its ancient
glass, and a comparison of the unity
of effect there experienced with the
internecine struggle exhibited in most
buildings furnished by the glass
painters of to-day, will surely con-
vince the most indifferent that there
is yet much to be learnt.

Secondly. The great difference between coloured glass and painted glass
must be kept in view. " *Coloured glass*
is obtained by a mixture of metallic
oxides whilst in a state of fusion. This
colouring pervades the substance of the
glass and becomes incorporated with
it." It is termed " pot metal." " To
paint glass the artist uses a plate of
translucent glass, and applies the design and colouring with vitrifiable
colours. These colours, true enamels,
are the product of metallic oxides
combined with vitreous compounds
called fluxes. Through the medium
of these, assisted by a strong heat, the
colouring matters are fixed upon the
plate of glass."[1]

In the window made of coloured

[1] " Industrial Arts. Historical Sketches,"
p. 195. Published for the Committee of Council
on Education. Chapman and Hall.

glass we have the material itself dyed with the richest tints in its full substance, the different pieces being held together by lead lines, and forming a species of translucent mosaic. Some details are painted and burnt on, but the main effect of the work is obtained by the rich colours of the pot-metal itself contrasted with the pearly tones of the clear glass. In the painted window translucency is nearly lost. Shadows are obtained by loading with enamel colours, and at the best the painted window becomes an indifferent picture badly placed.

In the painted window the lead lines, without which the various pieces of glass can not be held together, are, as far as possible, concealed. In the stained window the craftsman makes them his servant, and uses them as a means of giving additional richness of effect. They form an integral part of the design.

SOMERS CLARKE.

D

IX. TABLE GLASS.

Few materials lend themselves more readily to the skill of the craftsman than glass. The fluid or viscous condition of the "metal" as it comes from the "pot," the way in which it is shaped by the breath of the craftsman, and by his skill in making use of centrifugal force, these and many other things too numerous to mention are all manifested in the triumphs of the Venetian glass blower. At the first glance we see that the vessel he has made is of a material once liquid. He takes the fullest advantage of the conditions under which he works, and the result is a beautiful thing which can be produced in but one way.

For many centuries the old methods were followed, but with the power to produce the "metal," or glass of extreme purity and transparency, came the desire to leave the old paths, and produce work in imitation of crystal. The wheel came into play, and cut and engraved glass became general. At first there was nothing but a

genuine advance or variation on the
old modes.

The specimens of clear glass made
at the end of the seventeenth, and beginning of the eighteenth centuries,
are well designed to suit the capabilities of the material. The form
given to the liquid metal by the
craftsman's skill is still manifest, its
delicate transparency accentuated
here and there by cutting the surface
into small facets, or engraving upon
it graceful designs; but as skill in-
creased so taste degraded. The
graceful outlines and natural curves
of the old workers gave place to dis-
tortions of line but too common in
all decorative works of the period.
A little later and the material was
produced in mere lumps, cut and
tormented into a thousand surfaces,
suggesting that the work was made
from the solid, as, in part, it was.
This miserable stuff reached its
climax in the early years of the
present reign.

Since then a great reaction has
taken place. For example, the old
decanter, a massive lump of mis-
shapen material better suited to the
purpose of braining a burglar than

decorating a table, has given place to a light and gracefully formed vessel, covered in many cases with well designed surface engraving, and thoroughly suited both to the uses it is intended to fulfil and the material of which it is made. And not only so, but a distinct variation and development upon the old types has been made. The works produced have not been merely copies, but they have their own character. It is not necessary to describe the craft of the glass blower. It is sufficient to say that he deals with a material which, when it comes to his hands, is a liquid, solidifying rapidly on exposure to the air; that there is hardly a limit to the delicacy of the film that can be made; and, in addition to using a material of one colour, different colours can be laid one over the other, the outer ones being afterwards cut through by the wheel, leaving a pattern in one colour on a ground of another.

There has developed itself of late an unfortunate tendency to stray from the path of improvement,[1] but a

[1] Novelty rather than improvement is the rock on which our craftsmen are but too often wrecked.

due consideration on the part both of
the purchaser and of the craftsman of
how the material should be used will
result, it may be hoped, in farther
advances on the right road.

SOMERS CLARKE.

X. PRINTING.

Printing, in the only sense with
which we are at present concerned,
differs from most if not from all the
arts and crafts represented in the
Exhibition in being comparatively
modern. For although the Chinese
took impressions from wood blocks
engraved in relief for centuries before
the wood-cutters of the Netherlands,
by a similar process, produced the
block books, which were the immediate
predecessors of the true printed book,
the invention of moveable metal letters
in the middle of the fifteenth century
may justly be considered as the invention of the art of printing. And it
is worth mention in passing, that as
an example of fine typography, the
earliest printed book, the Gutenberg
Bible of 1450, has never been sur-

passed. Printing, then, for our purpose, may be considered as the art of
making books by means of moveable
types. Now, as all books not primarily
intended as picture - books consist
principally of types composed to form
letterpress, it is of the first importance
that the letter used should be fine in
form ; especially, as no more time is
occupied, or cost incurred, in casting,
setting, or printing beautiful letters,
than in the same operations with ugly
ones. So we find the fifteenth and
early sixteenth century printers, who
were generally their own type-foun-
ders, gave great attention to the forms
of their types. The designers of the
letters used in the earliest books were
probably the scribes whose manuscripts
the fifteenth century printed books so
much resemble. Aldus of Venice employed Francesco Francia of Bologna,
goldsmith and painter, to cut the
punches for his celebrated italic letter.
Froben, the great Basle printer, got
Holbein to design ornaments for his
press, and it is not unreasonable to
suppose that the painter may have
drawn the models for the noble
Roman types we find in Froben's
books. With the decadence in hand-

writing which became marked in the
sixteenth century, a change corresponding took place in the types; the
designers, no longer having beautiful
writing as a model and reference,
introduced variations arbitrarily. The
types of the Elzevirs are regular and
neat, and in this respect modern, but
they altogether lack the spirit and
originality that distinguish the early
Roman founts of Italy and Germany,
Gothic characteristics inherited from
their mediæval predecessors. In the
seventeenth century type-founding
began to be carried on as a craft apart
from that of the printer, and although
in this and in the succeeding century
many attempts were made to improve
the "face" (as the printing surface of
type is called), such examples as a
rule reflect only too clearly the growing debasement of the crafts of design.
Notable among these attempts were the
founts cut by William Caslon, who
started in business in London as a letter-
founder in 1720, taking for his models
the Elzevir types. [The last sentence
is set in a type of Caslon's.] From this
time until the end of the century he
and his successors turned out many
founts relatively admirable. But at

the end of the eighteenth century a
revolution was made, and the founders
entirely abandoned the traditional forms
of their predecessors, and evolved the
tasteless letters with which nearly
all the books published during the
first sixty years of the present century
are printed, and which are still almost
universally used for newspapers and
for Government publications. Par-
ticularly objectionable forms are in
every day use in all continental
countries requiring Roman letter.
[The last two sentences are set in a
type of this character.]

In 1844 the Chiswick Press printed
for Messrs. Longmans "The Diary of
Lady Willoughby," and revived for
this purpose one of Caslon's founts.
This was an important step in the
right direction, and its success induced
Messrs. Miller and Richard of Edin-
burgh to engrave a series of "old
style" founts, with one of which this
catalogue is printed. Most other
typefounders now cast similar type,
and without doubt if their customers,
the printers, demanded it, they would
expend some of the energy and talent,
which now go to cutting Japanese-
American and sham seventeenth cen-

tury monstrosities, in endeavouring
to produce once more the restrained
and beautiful forms of the early printers, until the day when the current
hand-writing may be elegant enough
to be again used as a model for the
type-punch engraver.

Next in importance to the type are
the ornaments, initial letters, and other
decorations which can be printed
along with it. These, it is obvious,
should always be designed and engraved so as to harmonize with the
printed page regarded as a whole.
Hence illustrations drawn only with
reference to purely pictorial effects are
entirely out of place in a book, that
is, if we desire seriously to make it
beautiful.

EMERY WALKER.

XI. BOOKBINDING.

Modern Bookbinding dates from the
application of printing to literature,
and in essentials has remained un-
changed to the present day, though
in those outward characteristics, which
appeal to the touch and to the eye,

and constitute Binding in an artistic sense, it has gone through many changes for better and for worse, which, in the opinion of the writer, have resulted, in the main, in the exaggeration of technical skill and in the death of artistic fancy.

The first operation of the modern binder is to fold or re-fold the printed sheet into a section, and to gather the sections, numbered or lettered at the foot, in their proper order into a volume.

The sections are then taken, one by one, placed face downwards in a frame, and sewn through the back by a continuous thread running backwards and forwards along the backs of the sections to upright strings fastened at regular intervals in the sewing frame.

This process unites the sections to one another in series one after the other, and permits the perusal of the book by the simple turning of leaf after leaf upon the hinge formed by the thread and the back of the section.

A volume, or series of sections, so treated, the ends of the string being properly secured, is essentially

"bound"; all that is subsequently
done is done for the protection or for
the decoration of the volume or of its
cover.

The sides of a volume are protected
by millboards, called shortly "boards."
The boards themselves and the back
are protected by a cover of leather,
vellum, silk, linen, or paper, wholly or
in part. The edges of the volume are
protected by the projection of the
boards beyond them at top, bottom,
and fore-edge, and usually by being
cut smooth and gilt.

A volume so bound and protected
may be decorated by tooling or otherwise upon all the exposed surfaces—
upon the edges, the sides, and the
back—and may be designated by
lettering upon the back or the sides.

The degree in which a bound book
is protected and decorated will deter-
mine the class to which the binding
will belong.

(1) In *cloth binding* the cover,
called a "case," is made apart from the
book, and is attached as a whole after
the book is sewn.

(2) In *half binding* the cover is built
up for and on each individual book,
but the boards of which it is composed

are only partly covered with the
leather or other material which covers
the back.

(3) In *whole binding* the boards are
wholly covered with leather or other
durable material, which in half binding
covers only a portion of them.

(4) In *extra binding* whole binding
is advanced a stage higher by decoration. Of course in the various stages
the details vary commensurately with
the stage itself, being more or less
elaborate as the stage is higher or
lower in the scale.

The process of *extra binding* set
out in more detail is as follows :—

(1) First the sections are folded or
refolded.

(2) Then, " end-papers "—sections
of plain paper added at the beginning
and end of the volume to protect the
first and last, the most exposed, sections of printed matter constituting
the volume proper—having been prepared and added, the sections are
beaten, or rolled, or pressed, to make
them " solid."

The end-papers are usually added
at a later stage, and are pasted on,
and not sewn, but, in the opinion of
the writer, it is better to add them at

this stage, and to sew them and not to paste them.

(3) Then the sections are sewn as already described.

(4) When sewn the volume passes into the hands of the "forwarder," who

(5) "Makes" the back, beating it round, if the back is to be round, and "backing" it, or making it fan out from the centre to right and left and project at the edges to form a kind of ridge to receive and to protect the edges of the boards which form the sides of the cover.

(6) The back having been made, the "boards" (made of millboard, and originally of wood) for the protection of the sides are made and cut to shape, and attached by lacing into them the ends of the strings upon which the book has been sewn.

(7) The boards having been attached, the edges of the book are now cut smooth and even at the top, bottom, and fore-edge, the edges of the boards being used as guides for the purpose. In some cases the order is reversed, and the edges are first cut and then the boards.

(8) The edges may now be coloured and gilt, and if it is proposed to "gauf-

fer" or to decorate them with tooling, they are so treated at this stage.

(9) The head-band is next worked on at head and tail, and the back lined with paper or leather or other material to keep the head-band in its place and to strengthen the back itself.

The book is now ready to be covered.

(10) If the book is covered with leather, the leather is carefully pared all round the edges and along the line of the back, to make the edges sharp and the joints free.

(11) The book having been covered, the depression on the inside of the boards caused by the overlap of the leather is filled in with paper, so that the entire inner surface may be smooth and even, and ready to receive the first and last leaves of the end-papers, which finally are cut to shape and pasted down, leaving the borders only uncovered.

Sometimes, however, the first and last leaves of the "end-papers" are of silk, and the "joint" of leather, in which case, of course, the end-papers are not pasted down, but the insides of the boards are independently treated, and are covered, sometimes with leather, sometimes with silk or other material.

The book is now "forwarded," and passes into the hands of the "finisher" to be tooled or decorated, or "finished" as it is called.

The decoration in gold on the surface of leather is wrought out, bit by bit, by means of small brass stamps called "tools."

The steps of the process are shortly as follows :—

(12) The pattern having been settled and worked out on paper, it is "transferred" to, or marked out on, the various surfaces to which it is to be applied.

Each surface is then prepared in succession, and, if large, bit by bit, to receive the gold.

(13) First the leather is washed with water or with vinegar.

(14) Then the pattern is pencilled over with "glaire" (white of egg beaten up and drained off), or the surface is wholly washed with it.

(15) Next it is smeared lightly with grease or oil.

(16) And, finally, the gold (gold leaf) is applied by a pad of cotton wool, or a flat thin brush called a "tip."

(17) The pattern, visible through the gold, is now reimpressed or worked

with the tools heated to about the temperature of boiling water, and the unimpressed or waste gold is removed by an oiled rag, leaving the pattern in gold and the rest of the leather clear.

These several operations are, in England, usually distributed among five classes of persons.

(1) The *superintendent* or person responsible for the whole work.

(2) The *sewer*, usually a woman, who folds, sews, and makes the head-bands.

(3) The *book-edge gilder*, who gilds the edges.   Usually a craft apart.

(4) The *forwarder*, who performs all the other operations leading up to the finishing.

(5) The *finisher*, who decorates and letters the volume after it is forwarded.

In Paris the work is still further distributed, a special workman (*couvreur*) being employed to prepare the leather for covering and to cover.

In the opinion of the writer the work, as a craft of Beauty, suffers, as do the workmen, from the allocation of different operations to different workmen.   The work should be conceived of as one, and be wholly executed by one person, or at most by two, and especially should there be no distinction between "finisher" and "forwarder," between "executant" and "artist."

The following technical names may serve to call attention to the principal features of a bound book.

(1) *The back*, the posterior edge of the volume upon which at the present time the title is usually placed. Formerly it was placed on the fore-edge or side.

The back may be (*a*) convex or concave or flat; (*b*) marked horizontally with bands, or smooth from head to tail; (*c*) tight, the leather or other covering adhering to the back itself, or hollow, the leather or other covering not so adhering; and (*d*) stiff or flexible.

(2) *Edges*, the three other edges of the book,—the top, the bottom, and the fore-edge.

(3) *Bands*, the cords upon which the book is sewn, and which, if not "let in" or imbedded in the back, appear on it as parallel ridges. The ridges are, however, usually artificial, the real

bands being "let in" to facilitate the sewing, and their places supplied by thin slips of leather cut to resemble them and glued on the back. This process also enables the forwarder to give great sharpness and finish to this part of his work, if he think it worth while.

(4) *Between-bands*, the space between the bands.

(5) *Head* and *tail*, the top and bottom of the back.

(6) The *head-band* and *head-cap*, the fillet of silk worked in buttonhole stitch at the head and tail, and the cap or cover of leather over it. The head-band had its origin probably in the desire to strengthen the back and to resist the strain when a book is pulled by head or tail from the shelf.

(7) *Boards*, the sides of the cover, stiff or limp, thick or thin, in all degrees.

(8) *Squares*, the projection of the boards beyond the edges of the book. These may be shallow or deep in all degrees, limited only by the purpose they have to fulfil and the danger they will themselves be exposed to if too deep.

(9) *Borders*, the overlaps of leather on the insides of the boards.

(10) *Proof*, the rough edges of leaves left uncut in cutting the edges to show where the original margin was, and to prove that the cutting has not been too severe.

The life of bookbinding is in the dainty mutation of its mutable elements—back, bands, boards, squares, decoration. These elements admit of almost endless variation, singly and in combination, in kind and in degree. In fact, however, they are now almost always uniformly treated or worked up to one type or set of types. This is the death of bookbinding as a craft of beauty.

The finish, moreover, or execution, has outrun invention, and is the great characteristic of modern bookbinding. This again, the inversion of the due order, is, in the opinion of the writer, but as the carving on the tomb of a dead art, and itself dead.

A well-bound beautiful book is neither of one type, nor finished so that its highest praise is that " had it been made by a machine it could not have been made better." It is individual; it is instinct with the hand of

him who made it ; it is pleasant to feel,
to handle, and to see ; it is the original
work of an original mind working in
freedom simultaneously with hand and
heart and brain to produce a thing of
use, which all time shall agree ever
more and more also to call "a thing
of beauty."

T. J. COBDEN-SANDERSON.

CATALOGUE

NOTES.

It must be understood that the copyright of all designs in this Exhibition is reserved, and sketching is not allowed without written permission.

Where the exhibitor of a work is also the designer and executant the name is not repeated.

The utmost pains have been taken to make the Catalogue correspond to the intentions of the Society, and, if any Artist or Crafts-man is omitted where he ought to be men-tioned, the Society hopes he will bear in mind the difficulty of a first attempt, and excuse it.

The Society does not undertake the sale of any work, but prices may be obtained from the Secretary at the table, who will also put intending purchasers in communication with the artists.

The Exhibition is open, Sundays excepted, from 10 a.m. to 7 p.m. Admission 1s. On and after Saturday, the 10th Nov., with the exception (1) of Tuesday night, the 13th, and (2) of Thursday (Lecture) nights, the Exhibi-tion will be open to the public, at the reduced price of 6d., on the evenings of week-days from 7 p.m. to 10 p.m. On Sunday, the 4th Nov., and Sunday, the 18th Nov., the Exhi-bition will be open, free (by ticket) to the public, from 3 p.m. to 9 p.m. Tickets to be had of Mark H. Judge, Esq., Hon. Sec. Sunday Society, 8, Park Place Villas, W., or at the Gallery.

The Exhibition closes finally on Decem-ber 1st.

WEST GALLERY.

C. F. A. VOYSEY.

1. Design for Printed Curtain : to be printed on silk, cotton, or wool.

2. Design for Cretonne : to be printed on cotton or silk.

3. Design for Cretonne or Printed Silk : to be printed on silk, cotton, or wool.

E. A. HOLMES.

4. Frame of Lace. Pillow lace with raised work on both sides, and Dresden point.

UNA TAYLOR.

5. Frame of Embroidery : in silk.

RIGBY AND RIGBY.

6. Design for Paper-hanging.

J. D. SEDDING.

7. Design for a Table Cover, &c.

MARY A. SMITH.
8. Embroidery in Needlework on Langdale Linen.

DORA STEWART.
9. Design for wall paper.

ANNIE NEWBOLD.
10. Design for wall paper.

MRS. ALDAM HEATON.
11. Screen Panel: embroidered on cloth in "tram" silk: the ground being embroidered as well as the design.
Designed by JOHN ALDAM HEATON.

FANNY CARR.
12. Table Cover, in silk on plush.

MRS. HOLIDAY.
13. Silk Portière: in darning work.
Designed and executed by HENRY and CATHERINE HOLIDAY.

DORA STEWART.
14. Design for Wall Paper.

CLEMENT HEATON.
15. Embossed Leather.

MRS. ALDAM HEATON.

16. Screen Panel: embroidered on cloth in "tram" silk : the ground being embroidered as well as the design.
Designed by JOHN ALDAM HEATON.

W. DE MORGAN.

17. Decorative Panel in Tiles.
Painted for the Princess de Scey Montbéliard, for wall of conservatory
Designed by W. DE MORGAN.

A. M. LUCAS.

18. Tapestry Work in silk.
Design adapted from old Italian work.
Executed by A. M. LUCAS.

UNA TAYLOR.

19. Embroidered Panel : on silk.
Designed by E. H. STEPHENS.
Executed by UNA TAYLOR.
19a. Chalice Veil.

MRS. CRANE.

20. Frieze for mantel valance :
worked in cotton on black merino.
Designed by WALTER CRANE.
Executed by MRS. CRANE.

E

MARY BUCKLE.

21. Satin Panel: peacock's feather embroidered in floss silk.

MRS. ERNEST HART.

21 a. Miniature Frames with silk embroidered panels.

Designed by UNA TAYLOR.

Executed by EMPLOYÉS OF THE DONEGAL INDUSTRIAL FUND.

MRS. M. MACARTNEY.

22. Needlework panel in crewels after A. Durer.

HEYWOOD SUMNER.

23. Panels for door of corner cupboard.

24. Panel: "St. George and the Dragon."

Both panels incised by C. H. WATTON.

HERBERT COLE.

25. Border: in silk embroidery.

MARGARET ASHWORTH.

26. Covering for a Grand piano: in twilled linen. The design outlined in crewel stitch: the ground work darned in silk.

Design copied from an ancient piece of German tapestry.

Executed by MARGARET ASHWORTH.

MRS. CRANE.

27. Cabinet: in ebonized wood, with needlework panels.

Designed by WALTER CRANE.

Executed by MARY FRANCES CRANE.

Cabinet work by C. HUNT and C. LUMLEY.

MRS. AGLAIA CORONIO.

27 a. Screen: mother-of-pearl with silk embroidery.

27 b. Box: mother-of-pearl with embroidery.

CALLIOPE CORONIO.

27 c. Paper-case and blotter: in pearl and wood, hand-painted.

MRS. CRANE.

28. Band for waist: on cloth and in cotton.

Designed by WALTER CRANE.

29 & 30. Hanging memoranda

pockets : worked in wool and crewels
on canvas.

Designed by WALTER CRANE.

J. ELLIOTT.

31.   Design for a Frieze.

ANDREW B. DONALDSON.

32.   Panel : in oil-colour, two tints,
for a nursery cupboard.

33.   Panel for a Room (representing a view of Groningen) : in oil-
colour tints of reddish brown.

MRS. R. BATEMAN.

33 a.   Panel : in silk on linen.
Designed by ROBERT BATEMAN.
Worked by MRS. R. BATEMAN.

W. A. S. BENSON.

34.   Arcaded screen : carved wood.
Designed by W. A. S. BENSON.
Executed by J. MCVEIGH.

35 & 36.   Pair of finger plates : in
copper repoussé.
Designed by HEYWOOD SUMNER.
Executed by J. MURTHWAITE,
Eyot Metal Works.

MRS. ERNEST HART.

36 a. Appliqué work in " Kells " coloured linens.

Design after Persian work.

Executed by A CLASS OF IRISH GIRLS.

JOHN ALDAM HEATON.

37. Patent Axminster carpet : wool pile. A careful reproduction of old Persian work.

Executed by TEMPLETON AND CO.

38. Chimney - piece in American walnut: frieze painted on mahogany.

Designed by J. ALDAM HEATON.

The frieze executed by EDWARD INGRAM TAYLOR.

The grate by LONGDEN AND CO., and the tiles by F. GARRARD.

39. Axminster carpet, wool pile : a "surround" for a billiard table. A careful reproduction of old Persian work.

Executed by TEMPLETON AND CO.

40. Wall paper : stencilled in transparent oil-colour on a ground of transparent water-colour.

41. Decorative panel : raised in gesso (gilt and partly painted), on a panel of stained and polished wood.

JOHN ALDAM HEATON—*continued.*
Design adapted by J. ALDAM HEATON.

Painted by J. ALDAM HEATON.

The gesso work by W. B. CHAMPION.

42. Marqueterie panel for a Cabinet.

43. Marqueterie panel for Cabinet: inlaid in dyed, stained and burnt wood, and mother-of-pearl.

Designed by J. ALDAM HEATON.

Executed by E. WILLIAMS.

44. Mirror frame: embroidered on cloth in "tram" silk : the ground being embroidered as well as the design.

Designed by JOHN ALDAM HEATON.

Executed by MRS. ALDAM HEATON.

45. Marqueterie: frieze and panels of a cabinet : inlaid in dyed, stained, and burnt wood.

Designed by J. ALDAM HEATON.

Executed by E. WILLIAMS.

46. Wall paper : stencilled in transparent oil-colour on a ground of transparent water-colour.

47. Marqueterie panel: unfinished : not engraved, shaded, or polished.

JOHN ALDAM HEATON—*continued.*

48. Decorative panel : raised in gesso (gilt and partly painted) on a panel of stained and polished wood.
Designed and painted by J. AL-DAM HEATON.
The gesso work by W. B. CHAMPION.

49. Leaf of a folding screen : painted in oils on silvered and lacquered sheepskin.
Designed by J. ALDAM HEATON.
Executed by ELLEN STEADMAN.

MORRIS AND CO.

50. Inlaid mahogany cabinet.
Designed by G. JACK.
Executed by H. SIDWELL and W. THATCHER.

50 a. Cotton velvets : block printed.
Designed by WILLIAM MORRIS.
Executed by MORRIS AND CO.

50 b. Hammersmith carpet : wool, hand-made.
Designed by WILLIAM MORRIS.
Executed by MORRIS AND CO.

50 c. "Arras" tapestry : woven in the high warp loom.

MORRIS AND CO.—*continued.*

Designed by PHILIP WEBB, H. DEARLE, and WILLIAM MORRIS.

Executed by CHARLES KNIGHT and JOHN SLEATH.

50 d. Eight specimens of silk damask : hand-woven.

Designed by WILLIAM MORRIS.

Executed by MORRIS AND CO.

50 e. Screen : Tulip and Pomegranate embroidered with floss silk.

Designed and executed by MAY MORRIS.

50 f. " Arras " tapestry : " St. Cecilia " : woven in the high warp loom.

Figure after E. BURNE-JONES, A.R.A., background designed by H. DEARLE.

Executed by JOHN SLEATH.

50 g. Inlaid mahogany sideboard.

Designed by G. JACK.

Executed by H. SIDWELL and W. THATCHER.

50 h. " Arras " tapestry : " The Woodpecker " : woven in the high warp loom.

Designed by WILLIAM MORRIS.

Executed by CHARLES KNIGHT and JOHN SLEATH.

F. GARRARD.

51. Tiles for walls, hearths, etc.: in buff clay, coloured with transparent glazes and opaque enamels.

HEATON'S CLOISONNÉ MOSAIC L^D.

51 a. Decoration for pilaster: hand wrought.

Design adapted from Mediæval design by CLEMENT HEATON.

THOMAS WARDLE.

52. Specimens of silk and other fabrics.

Collection of printed crétonnes, cotton velvets, linens, challets, silk damasks, silk plushes, and Tussur silk plushes.

Ancient and modern designs, printed in permanent colours, some of them Eastern.

Colouring by THOMAS WARDLE.

LEEK EMBROIDERY SOCIETY.

52 a. A case of Leek embroidery.

Embroideries on Tussur silk, worked with the Indian wild silk. Designs chiefly Indian.

E 2

WALTER CRANE.

52 b. Frieze in plaster: "Arts and Crafts."

Designed by WALTER CRANE.

Modelled by WALTER CRANE and OSMUND WEEKS.

Cast by OSMUND WEEKS and WILLIAM FLAVETT.

52 c. Frieze panel in plaster : "Peacock and Crane."

Modelled and cast by OSMUND WEEKS.

52 d. Frieze panel in plaster : "Monkey and Dolphin."

Modelled and cast by OSMUND WEEKS.

JANET A. STUART MACGOUN.

52 e. Design for wall paper or Madras muslin: painted on tracing paper.

K. M. NUTTER.

52 f. Design for Tempera wall paper for cottage bedroom.

52 g. Design for Tempera wall paper for cottage bedroom.

J. D. SEDDING.

52 h. Design for the "Westminster" wall paper.

W. DE MORGAN.

53. Chimney-piece, hearth, and tiles.

Chimney-piece designed by HAL-SEY RICARDO.

Tiles in ship panel designed by W. DE MORGAN : painted by F. PASSENGER.

53 a. Vase.

Designed by W. DE MORGAN.

Thrown by R. HODKIN.

Painted by F. PASSENGER.

FRANK PORTER.

54. Design for a carpet.

F. PATON BROWN.

55. Designs for wall paper.

B. F. GAST.

56. " A Water Frolic : " study of line in two colours for paper or fabric.

CHARLOTTE H. SPIERS.

57. Wall paper.

WM. WOOLLAMS AND CO.

58. Design for wall paper : "Lecco."

Designed by LOUISA AUMONIER.

Executed by WM. WOOLLAMS AND Co.

OWEN W. DAVIS.

59. Ceiling diaper : " Northampton." Raised flock paper, block printed.

Designed by OWEN W. DAVIS.

Executed by WM. WOOLLAMS AND CO.

WM. WOOLLAMS AND CO.

60. Ceiling paper : "Takino."

Designed by G. C. HAITÉ.

Executed by WM. WOOLLAMS AND CO.

JEFFREY AND CO.

61. Wall paper : " The Jacobean " : printed by blocks on talc ground.

Designed by J. D. SEDDING.

62. Wall Paper : " The Westminster" : printed by blocks in colours and bronze.

Designed by J. D. SEDDING.

63. Embossed leather paper : hand-painted on lacquered metal ground.

Designed by J. D. SEDDING.

64. Embossed leather : hand-painted on lacquered silver.

Designed by J. D. SEDDING.

JEFFREY AND CO.—*continued.*

65. Embossed leather paper:
"The Golden Age": hand-painted on
lacquered metal ground.
Designed by WALTER CRANE.

66. Design for "The Golden
Age" for embossed leather paper.
Designed by WALTER CRANE.

67. Embossed leather: "The
Golden Age." Painted by hand on
lacquered silver.
Designed by WALTER CRANE.

68. Repoussé plate for "The
Golden Age."
Designed by WALTER CRANE.
Executed by THOMAS GODFREY.

69. Wall decoration : "The Wood-
notes," printed in coloured flocks
on flock ground.

> "Under the greenwood tree
> Who loves to lie with me,
> And tune his merry note
> Unto the sweet bird's throat."
>   W. SHAKESPEARE,
>   *As You Like It.*

Designed by WALTER CRANE.
Printed by ROBERT HITCHCOCK.

JEFFREY AND CO.—*continued.*

70. Leather Portière: "Arbor Vitæ," embossed and hand painted on lacquered silver.

Designed by WALTER CRANE.

71. Wall paper: "The Thistle Scroll," block printed in colours.

Designed by LEWIS F. DAY.

72. Wall paper: "Scroll and Flowers," block printed in colours.

Designed by LEWIS F. DAY.

73. Design for embossed leather paper: "The Arabesque."

Designed by LEWIS F. DAY.

74. Embossed leather: "The Arabesque," hand painted on lacquered silver.

Designed by LEWIS F. DAY.

75. Embossed leather paper: "The Arabesque," hand-painted on lacquered metal ground.

Designed by LEWIS F. DAY.

76. Copper repoussé plate for "The Arabesque."

Designed by LEWIS F. DAY.

Executed by THOMAS GODFREY.

77. Ceiling paper: block-printed in colour.

Designed by LEWIS F. DAY.

JEFFREY AND CO.—*continued.*

78. Wall paper: "Frieze": block-printed in colours.
Designed by LEWIS F. DAY.

79. Wall paper: block-printed in colours.
Designed by LEWIS F. DAY.

80. Drawing for a Ceiling and Frieze in embossed leather paper.
Drawn and designed by G. E. FOX.

81. Embossed Frieze on leather paper: hand-painted.
Designed by G. E. FOX.

82. Design of "Chrysanthemum Frieze."
Designed by W. J. MUCKLEY.

83. Wall paper: The "Chrysanthemum Frieze." Block-printed in colours.
Designed by W. J. MUCKLEY.

The specimens were printed under the direction of METFORD WARNER.

WM. WOOLLAMS AND CO.
85. "Savoy": ceiling paper: "Burke": block printed.
Designed by H. W. BEAVEN.
Executed by WM. WOOLLAMS AND CO.

WM. WOOLLAMS AND CO.—*contd.*

86. Wall paper: block printed.

Designed by A. F. BROPHY.

Executed by WM. WOOLLAMS AND CO.

87. "Cattaneo": wall paper: flock on mica ground: block printed.

Designed by C. F. A. VOYSEY.

Executed by WM. WOOLLAMS AND CO.

S. G. MAWSON.

88. Wall paper: "The Woodpecker."

Designed by S. G. MAWSON.

Executed by JEFFREY AND CO.

OWEN W. DAVIS.

89. Dado decoration in paper: "Grosvenor." (Adam's style.) Block printed.

Designed by OWEN W. DAVIS.

Executed by WM. WOOLLAMS AND CO.

GEO. C. HAITÉ.

90. Pomegranate Frieze: design for wall paper. Four colours. Block printed by hand.

Designed by GEO. C. HAITÉ.

Executed by SCOTT AND CUTHBERTSON.

GEO. C. HAITÉ—*continued.*
91. Frieze, "Picotee," in paper-hanging : block printed.
Designed by G. C. HAITÉ.
' Executed by WM. WOOLLAMS AND Co.

WM. WOOLLAMS AND CO.
92. Wall paper. "Fig": block printed.
Designed by A. SILVER.

JAMES LATTIMER.
93. Cotton Hanging : printed : "Wheatear in Clover."
Designed by JAMES LATTIMER.
Executed by

WM. WOOLLAMS AND CO.
94. Wall paper: "Savoy": block printed.
Designed by A. F. BROPHY.
Executed by WM. WOOLLAMS AND Co.

95. Wall paper: "Orchid": block printed.
Designed by G. C. HAITÉ.
Executed by WM. WOOLLAMS AND Co.

96. Wall paper: "Siri": block printed.

WM. WOOLLAMS AND CO.—*contd.*
Designed by F. J. WEIDEMANN.
Executed by WM. WOOLLAMS AND
CO.

TURNBULL AND STOCKDALE.

97. Reversible and other Cretonnes : roller printed.
Designed by LEWIS F. DAY.
Executed by TURNBULL AND
STOCKDALE.

REGINALD T. BLOMFIELD.

98. Gas Lantern : standard in wrought iron and brass.
Designed by REGINALD T. BLOMFIELD.
Executed at the Portland Metal Works.

98. Models of oak capitals : cast in plaster from clay.
Designed by REGINALD T. BLOMFIELD.
Executed by JOSEPH WITCOMBE.

98. Grate: the panel and ornamental detail cast in brass, and worked up by hand, from models prepared by JOSEPH WITCOMBE and REGINALD T. BLOMFIELD.
Executed at the Portland Metal Works.

REGINALD T. BLOMFIELD—*continued.*
98. Models of oak spandrels: cast
in plaster from clay.
Designed by REGINALD T. BLOM-
FIELD.
Executed by JOSEPH WITCOMBE.

98. Drawings: (*a*) Sketch showing new Staircase at Haileybury for
which the Gas Lantern was designed.
(*b*) Photograph of Doorway at
Haileybury, showing carvings.
(*c*) Photograph of wrought iron
Gates at Haileybury.
Designed by REGINALD T. BLOM-
FIELD.
(*d*) Full size details of Grate.
(*e*) Full size details of Lantern.

98. Plaster Cast from clay model
of carving for wooden mantel-piece.
Drawn and designed by REGINALD
T. BLOMFIELD.
Executed by JOSEPH WITCOMBE.

W. A. S. BENSON.
99. Ash Sideboard.
Designed by W. A. S. BENSON.
Executed by C. ROGERS.

99a. Pendant Lamp (in brass and
copper) for Electric Light.

W. A. S. BENSON—*continued.*
  Designed by W. A. S. BENSON.
  Executed by J. LOVEGROVE.
  99 b.   Standard Lamp.
  Designed by W. A. S. BENSON.
  Executed by J. LOVEGROVE.
  99 c.   Pair of Copper Bowls.
  Designed by W. A. S. BENSON.
  Executed by J. LOVEGROVE.

SIDNEY G. MAWSON.
  100.   Cretonne : 4 colours, "Lily of the Valley."
    1 colour, " Globe Thistle."
    1 piece of silk.

W. DE MORGAN.
  101.   Pyramid of tiles.
  103.   Case of Pottery.

CASE (103 a—123) OF EMBROIDERIES AND BOOKBINDINGS.

MRS. ERNEST HART.
  103 a, b, c.   Embroideries executed by EMPLOYÉS OF THE DONEGAL INDUSTRIAL FUND.

ROGER DE COVERLY.
  104.   Blake's Poems, 4 vols. ; Milton, 3 vols. ; Boccaccio's Decameron ; Goethe's Faust : all bound in Calf, different styles.

ROGER DE COVERLY—*continued.*

105. Dante's Inferno, small 4to : bound in Morocco, and finished in the style of Grolier.

Forwarded by R. DE COVERLY, and finished by FREDERICK HARVEY.

106. New Testament, 4to : bound in Levant Morocco, and finished after a design by Roger Payne.

Forwarded by R. DE COVERLY, and finished by FREDERICK HARVEY.

107. Milton's Paradise Lost, small 4to : Mr. Pickering's reprint, bound in Morocco and finished after a design (Early Italian binding) in the possession of the late Mr. Pickering, Piccadilly.

Executed by R. DE COVERLY and the late JOHN BARRINGTON.

108. Xavier de Maistre, 3 vols. : bound in Morocco (Jansenist). Fanshawe's Poems : bound in Morocco extra. Rossetti's Works, vol. ii. : bound in pigskin.

Designed by R. DE COVERLY.

Forwarded by R. DE COVERLY, finished by FREDERICK HARVEY and the late JOHN BARRINGTON.

LORENZO DE COVERLY.

109. Stevenson's Inland Voyage:
bound in Morocco.

J. MOYR SMITH.

110. Cloth case for bookbinding.
Designed by J. MOYR SMITH.
Executed by

CHRISTOPHER W. WHALL.

111. Rush-plaiting design applied
to leather cases for bookbinding.
Designed by CHRISTOPHER W.
WHALL.
Blocks cut by STRAKER AND CO.
Cases covered by STEVENSON AND
CO.

LEWIS F. DAY.

112. Case for binding : cloth gilt.
Designed by LEWIS F. DAY.
Executed by MATTHEW BELL.

113. Case for binding : cloth gilt.
Designed by LEWIS F. DAY.
Executed by BURN AND CO.

JAMES BURN AND CO.

114. Cover or case for book :
cloth, decorated in gold.
Designed by the late DANTE
GABRIEL ROSSETTI.

JAMES BURN AND CO.—*continued.*
   115. Cover or case for book:
cloth, decorated in gold.
   Designed by PHILIP WEBB.
   116. Cover or case for book:
cloth, decorated in gold.
   Designed by MRS. ORRINSMITH.

EDWARD WATSON.
   117. Five Specimens of bookbinding in hand-coloured calf: an-
tique style and finish.
   Designed by EDWARD WATSON.
   Finished by GEORGE AYLING.

ROBERT RIVIERE AND SON.
   118. Bookbinding : in morocco
leather: hand tooled. (Marriage of
Cupid and Psyche. 1 vol.)
   Design original.
   Forwarded and covered by C. PER-
CIVAL.
   Finished by R. CORSTORPHIN.

   119. Bookbinding : in morocco
leather: hand tooled. (Marriage of
Cupid and Psyche. 1 vol.)
   Design original.
   Forwarded and covered by C. PER-
CIVAL.
   Finished by R. CORSTORPHIN.

RIVIERE AND SON—*continued.*

120. Bookbinding : in morocco leather : hand tooled. (Marriage of Cupid and Psyche. I vol.)
Design original.
Forwarded and covered by C. PER-CIVAL.
Finished by R. LEIGHTON.

GEORGE COFFEY.

121. "Congal," by Sir Samuel Ferguson.

122. "Poems," by Sir Samuel Ferguson.

123. "Parables of our Lord." Pictures by Sir J. E. Millais, R.A.
All bound in calf by JAMES SHER-WIN. Sewn by MARY ANNE O'HARA; Designs adapted from Early Irish and embossed by G. COFFEY.

CENTURY GUILD OF ARTISTS.

124. Hangings.
Designed by H. P. HORNE.

125. Brass lamp.
Designed by A. H. MACKMURDO.
Brass work executed by G. ES-LING : and the silhouettes by SME-THAM ALLEN.

CENTURY GUILD—*continued.*

126. Paper and frieze for Music-room.
Designed by HERBERT P. HORNE.
Executed by JEFFREY AND CO.

127. Embroidered screen.
Designed by A. H. MACKMURDO.
Executed by WILKINSON AND SONS.

128. Century Guild Cottage Piano.
Designed by A. H. MACKMURDO.
Executed by WILKINSON AND SONS.

129. Copper Panel for Sconce.
Designed and executed by KELLOCK BROWN.

130. Brass Sconce.
Designed by A. H. MACKMURDO.
Executed by G. ESLING.

131. Copper Sconce.
Designed and executed by KELLOCK BROWN.

132. Pair of brass candlesticks.
Designed by A. H. MACKMURDO.
Executed by G. ESLING.

133. Silhouette: suggestion for a design for decoration of a frieze or panel: cut in copper.

CENTURY GUILD—*continued.*
Designed and executed by SME-
THAM ALLEN.

134. Silhouette: suggestion for a
design for decoration of a frieze or
panel: cut in brass.
Designed and executed by SME-
THAM ALLEN.

135. Silhouette for screens,
shades, and inlaying: cut in paper.
Designed and executed by SME-
THAM ALLEN.

136. Silhouette for silver or
ivory: cut in paper.
Designed and executed by SME-
THAM ALLEN.

137 & 138. Silhouette for metal
frieze, or for inlaying in panels: cut
in metal. They are imbedded in
coloured cement, or laid over a metal
ground.
Designed and executed by SME-
THAM ALLEN.

139. Cabinet: for canopy as
shown in drawing.
Designed by A. H. MACKMURDO.
Cabinet work by POCOCK: Painting
by SELWYN IMAGE.

140. Bust: in Terra cotta.

CENTURY GUILD—*continued.*

141. Rug.
Designed by A. H. MACKMURDO.
Executed by WILKINSON AND SONS.

142. Stencilling in Oil on Water-colour ground.
The objects, top and bottom, left intentionally incomplete.
Designed by J. ALDAM HEATON.
Executed by ALFRED WHITE.

DECORATIVE NEEDLEWORK SOCIETY.

143. Case containing Needlework.

143 a. Portière embroidered in silk.

143 b. Wall panel.
Designed by MARY GEMMELL.

T. J. COBDEN-SANDERSON.

144. Case containing Specimens of Bookbinding in Morocco, wholly worked and tooled by hand:
(a) "The Prelude. 1850."
Lent by MISS RAVEN.
(b) "Memoir of Daniel Macmillan. 1882."
Lent by F. MACMILLAN, ESQ.
(c) "British Birds. Bewick. 1809."
Lent by MRS. HENRY HOLIDAY.

T. J. COBDEN-SANDERSON—*continued.*

(d) " Utopia. 1869."

(e) " The Life and Death of Jason. 1882."

(f) " Love is Enough. 1873."
Lent by F. S. ELLIS, ESQ.

(g) " Homeri Ilias. 1881."

(h) " Endymion. 1818."
Lent by F. S. ELLIS, ESQ.

(i) " Les Enfants. Paris."
Lent by the HON. MRS. STANLEY.

(k) " Sibylline Leaves. 1817."

(l) " The Defence of Guenevere. 1858."

(m) " Keats. 1884."
Lent by the COUNTESS DE GREY.

(n) " Macbeth, Hamlet, King Lear. 1883."

(o) " Unto this Last. 1884."

(p) " Romeo and Juliet, Hamlet."
Lent by MRS. MACKAIL.

(q) " The Gospels according to Matthew, Mark, and Luke. 1885."

(r) " The Two Paths. 18 ."
Lent by G. A. CRAWLEY, ESQ.

(s) " The Germ. 1850."
Lent by MRS. HENRY HOLIDAY.

T. J. COBDEN-SANDERSON—*continued.*
(t) "The Revolt of Islam. 1818."

Sewn by ANNIE COBDEN-SAN-DERSON.

Edges gilt by J. GWYNN.

Designed, forwarded, gauffered and finished by T. J. COBDEN-SANDERSON.

MAY MORRIS.

145. Silk embroidered cover for "Love is Enough."

Designed and embroidered by MAY MORRIS.

WILLIAM MORRIS.

146. Case of Illuminated MSS.
Lent by MRS. BURNE-JONES.

147. "The Story of the Dwellers in Eyr."

148. Leaves of "Odes of Horace."
The heads in the angles of the first page designed by E. BURNE-JONES.

149. "Rubaiyát of Omar Kháyyám."

150. "A Book of Verses."
Picture painted by C. F. MURRAY.
Coloured letters by GEO. WARDLE.
The rest of the ornament and the writing and the verses by WILLIAM MORRIS.

WALTER CRANE.

152. Tesserated Cartoon for mosaic frieze panel : repeat of two designs. Water-colour on tracing cloth.

153. Cartoon for a nursery wall paper : in water-colour on cartoon paper, representing " The House that Jack Built."

154. Tesserated Cartoon for mosaic frieze : water-colour on tracing cloth.

155. Tesserated design for mosaic frieze : water-colour on tracing cloth.

HEYWOOD SUMNER.

156. Drawings explaining sgraffito decoration.

157 & 158. Symbols in polychrome sgraffito : specimens of the sgraffito decoration of Llanvair Kilgeddin Church, Abergavenny.

H EYWOOD S UMNER—*continued.*
Designed and cut by H EYWOOD
S UMNER.
Plastered by J AS. W ILLIAMS.

159. Drawings explaining sgraffito decoration.

160. Cartoon design for sgraffito decoration of Llanvair Kilgeddin Church, Abergavenny. Subject, " O ye mountains and hills."

161. Cartoon design for sgraffito decoration of Llanvair Kilgeddin Church, Abergavenny. Subject, " O ye winds."

162. Photographs explaining the sgraffito decoration of Llanvair Kilgeddin Church.

HENRY HOLIDAY.

163 & 164. Cartoons for stained glass for the Cavendish Memorial.

165. Plaster bas-relief : " Jacob's Ladder."

166, a & b. Designs for glass : chalk drawing : Angels from " Jacob's Ladder."

167 & 168. Cartoons for glass, for the Cavendish Memorial.

FREDERICK J. SHIELDS.

169. Design for portion of the stained glass for the Duke of Westminster's Chapel at Eaton Hall, Cheshire.

E. BURNE-JONES.

170. Design for windows. "David's Exhortation to Solomon concerning the building of the Temple."

SELWYN IMAGE.

170 a. Crayon design for one of the lights of the Parish Church, Morthoe, North Devon : "Raphael."

170 b. Crayon design for glass window : "Michael."

HENRY HOLIDAY.

170 c. Design for glass : chalk drawing : "Music and Painting."

N. H. WESTLAKE.

171. Cartoon for a painting in the Chapel of Glossop Hall.
"Magnificat anima mea."

E. BURNE-JONES.

172. Cartoon for figure of S. Michael.

E. BURNE-JONES—*continued.*

173. Cartoon for window at S. Philip's Church, Birmingham : "The Nativity."

174. Cartoon for part of a mosaic executed at Murano for the Apse of the American Church of S. Paul, Rome.

175. Design for mosaic. " The Nativity."

176. Small photograph of the complete Apse.

177. Design for mosaic. " The Tree of Life."

178. A coloured sketch of the cartoon : " The Circle of Angels."

179. Design for mosaic. " The Annunciation."

180. Photographs of figures.
Uriel with the Sun.
Michael.
Gabriel.
Chemuel with a Chalice.
Zophiel with the Moon.

181. Cartoon for window : "The Crucifixion."
Companion picture to No. 173.

E. BURNE-JONES—*continued.*
182. Cartoon for figure of S. Gabriel.

HENRY HOLIDAY.
183, 184, 185, 185 a, 185 b, 185 c, 185 d, 185 e. Designs for stained glass.

E. I. TAYLOR.
186. Cartoon for stained glass.

CHRISTOPHER W. WHALL.
187. Four cartoons for stained glass.

HEYWOOD SUMNER.
187 a. Roundel in gesso for a screen in a church at Newcastle : silvered and tinted with lacquers.
Designed and lacquered by H. SUMNER : modelled by HEYWOOD SUMNER and OSMUND WEEKS.

WALTER CRANE.
187 b. "Fox and Crane." Frieze panel in fibrous plaster, silvered and tinted with lacquers.
Designed and coloured by WALTER CRANE : modelled and cast by OSMUND WEEKS.

WALTER CRANE—*continued.*

187 C. Lunette in fibrous plaster toned with lacquer : " The Lion in Love."

Designed by WALTER CRANE: modelled and cast by OSMUND WEEKS.

LEWIS F. DAY.

188. Signs of the Zodiac : panels painted on oak.

Designed and executed by LEWIS F. DAY and GEORGE McCULLOCH.

The actual drawing of the figure in other designs by the same Exhibitor is equally due to GEORGE McCULLOCH.

FREDERICK J. SHIELDS.

189. Design for stained glass.
" Gather ye together first the tares."

CENTURY GUILD OF ARTISTS.

190. " Haymaker " : Man with hay-pike : In plaster, for stone or terra cotta.

Designed and executed by B. CRESWICK.

WALTER CRANE.

190 a. Frieze panel in fibrous plaster: "The North Wind, the Sun, and the Traveller."

Designed and coloured with lacquers by WALTER CRANE: modelled and cast by OSMUND WEEKS.

HEYWOOD SUMNER.

190 b. Roundel in gesso for a screen in a church at Newcastle: silvered and tinted with lacquers.

Designed and coloured by HEYWOOD SUMNER: modelled by HEYWOOD SUMNER and OSMUND WEEKS.

CENTURY GUILD OF ARTISTS.

191. "A True Workman and Grinder": cast in plaster, for stone or terra cotta.

Designed and executed by B. CRESWICK.

192. Design for wood carving: marine subject.

Designed and executed by B. CRESWICK.

193 a. "The Village Smith": "Under a spreading chestnut tree." Plaster cast, for bronze.

CENTURY GUILD—*continued.*

Designed and executed by B. CRESWICK.

193 b. "The Village Smith":
"He goes on Sunday to the church."
Plaster cast, for bronze.

Designed and executed by B. CRESWICK.

193 c. "The Village Smith":
"The children coming home from
school
Look in at the open door."
Plaster cast, for bronze.

Designed and executed by B. CRESWICK.

WALTER CRANE.

194 & 195. Set of six sketches in colour, $1\frac{1}{2}$ in. scale, for a painted frieze illustrating the story of "The Skeleton in Armour" of Longfellow.

FORD MADOX BROWN.

196. Cartoon for stained glass.

CENTURY GUILD OF ARTISTS.

197. "Haymaker": Man with scythe: in plaster, for stone or terra cotta.

Designed and executed by B. CRESWICK.

LEWIS F. DAY.

198. Designs for stained glass and majolica.

199. Designs for illumination in stained glass and tapestry frieze.

200. Design for panel of a door.

201. Six designs for stained glass.

202. Design for a fan.

203. Eleven sketch designs for stained glass.

204. Seven sketch designs for stained glass.

F. HAMILTON JACKSON.
205. Cartoon for stained glass.

FREDERICK J. SHIELDS.
205 a. Design for a portion of the stained glass for the Duke of Westminster's Chapel at Eaton Hall.

WALTER CRANE.
206, 207, 208, & 209. Four cartoons for stained glass panels for a library window: in water-colour on cartoon paper.

CHRISTOPHER W. WHALL.

211. Water-colour cartoon for church window : Subject, " He took a little child and set him in the midst."

212. Water-colour sketch for domestic window : Subject, " Fire."

213. Water-colour cartoon for domestic window : Subject, "Water."

AVELING GREEN.

214. Fresco, " St. James": one of a series of figures for the Church of St. Gregory, Sudbury, Suffolk.

Executed in Gambier Parry's spirit method.

215. Photographs of six Apostles.

CHRISTOPHER W. WHALL.

216. Small design for glass. " The Elements."

217. Water-colour sketch for church window: Subject, "Preaching."

AVELING GREEN.

218. Fresco, " St. John ": one of a series of figures for the Church of St. Gregory, Sudbury, Suffolk.

Executed in Gambier Parry's spirit method.

Reductions from original designs.

WALTER CRANE.

219. Tesserated design for frieze panel in mosaic: " Sirens." Water-colour on cartoon paper.

The repeated ornamental parts drawn by HARRY LESLIE.

220. Design for wall paper.

221. Tesserated cartoon for mo-saic frieze panel: " Fire." Water-colour on tracing cloth.

222. Tesserated cartoon for mo-saic frieze panel: " Earth." Water-colour on tracing cloth.

E. BURNE-JONES.

223. Fragment of cartoon of Cherubim and Seraphim and Thrones round a figure of Christ holding the World.

WALTER CRANE.

224. Cartoon for frieze of wall paper: " Wood-notes." Water-colour on cartoon paper.

225. Cartoon for wall paper: " Wood-notes." Water-colour on car-toon paper.

226. Tesserated cartoon for mo-saic frieze panel: " Air." Water-colour on tracing cloth.

WALTER CRANE—*continued.*

227. Cartoon for mosaic. "Eagle and Snake."

228. Cartoon for mosaic. "Sphinx."

E. BURNE-JONES.

229. A Cassone in gesso, gilded and coloured.

"The Garden of the Hesperides."

Designed and painted by E. BURNE-JONES.

The cabinet work by CHARLES LUMLEY.

The gesso work by OSMUND WEEKS.

The words in the end panels from "The Life and Death of Jason," by WILLIAM MORRIS.

SCREEN.

SPENCER STANHOPE.

230. Hanging cupboard: painted and gilt.

MRS. C. WYLIE.

231. Panel in gesso duro: "Twilight."

A. KEIDEL.

232.   Bust of a Lady : in boxwood.

233.   Kittens : in boxwood.

H. J. L. J. MASSÉ.

233 a.   Blade for fish slice : in nickel (for electro silvering), pierced and chased.

Date of design about 1725.

Executed by H. J. L. J. MASSÉ.

THOMAS WALLACE HAY.

234.   Panel : in gesso.

HAMO THORNYCROFT, R.A.

235.   Plaster bas-relief : " Artemis."

CONRAD DRESSLER.

236.   Plaster cast : " Tethys."

HENRY HOLIDAY.

237.   Bronze bas-relief : " Nymph and Cupid."

HAMO THORNYCROFT, R.A.

238.   Bronze bas-relief.
" The ploughman homeward plods his
      weary way."

WALTER CRANE.

239.   Frieze panel in gesso, tinted with lacquer, representing St. George

WALTER CRANE—*continued.*
and Dragon. (Gesso is composed of plaster of Paris, glue, and cotton wool.)

240. Models in gesso duro for Bell Plate, Door Handles, and Key Escutcheons : modelled with a brush in gesso duro for electro silver, the bell handles for copper.
Executed by OSMUND WEEKS.
(Figures finished by WALTER CRANE.)

241. Cabinet panels : decorated with designs in gesso, tinted with lacquer.

242. Frieze and panels for fireplace : in plaster, silvered and lacquered.
Photograph of complete fireplace.

243. Models in gesso duro for finger plates.

G. W. BAYES.
244. Artillery horses : modelled in wax.

HEYWOOD SUMNER.
245. Gesso panel : painted : " Judith."

PHILIP WEBB.

246. Plaster casts: for frieze decoration.
Designed by PHILIP WEBB.

CHRISTOPHER W. WHALL.

247. Experiment in tinting sculpture: a crucifix.

MERVYN MACARTNEY.

248. Frieze decoration in plaster.
Designed by MERVYN MACARTNEY.
Executed by JOSEPH WITCOMBE.

CHRISTOPHER W. WHALL.

249. Experiment in tinting sculpture.

CENTURY GUILD OF ARTISTS.

250. Four plaster casts: decorative.
Designed and executed by B. CRESWICK.

251. Frieze in plaster for Cutler's Hall.

CONRAD DRESSLER.

252. Model in plaster, for knocker.

MRS. NEWMAN GELL.

254. Bas-relief in plaster.

CONRAD DRESSLER.

255. Plaster models of panels for stove.

(*Screen ends here.*)

MRS. W. DE MORGAN.

256. Head of Medusa: in bronze.

R. SPENCER STANHOPE.

257. " Andromeda " : relief in plaster.

GERALD C. HORSLEY.

258. Panels in gesso duro.
Designed by GERALD C. HORSLEY.
Executed by OSMUND WEEKS.

MARK ROGERS.

262. The Centurion : bust in terra cotta, mounted on carved wood.

263. Mrs. Mark Rogers : bust in terra cotta, mounted on carved wood.

JOHN WILSON.

264. Model in plaster for head in bronze.

MARK ROGERS.
265. "Hero": bust in terra cotta.

JOHN WILSON.
266. Model in plaster for head in bronze.

KATE FAULKNER.
266 a. Grand pianoforte, made by JOHN BROADWOOD AND SONS, in an oak case upon a stand.

Decoration in gesso designed and executed by MISS KATE FAULKNER.

Case maker, J. BANKS.

Cabinet makers, J. WILSON, W. GILLAM, S. HOLKARD, T. PEGG.

Sound board maker, W. ROBINSON.

Marker-off of scale, T. MEAD.

Key-makers, C. TILLSON, G. WOOLSTON.

Finisher of action, J. SHEPHERD.

Lent by A. IONIDES, ESQ.

ENTRANCE HALL.

HENRY HOLIDAY.
267. Mosaic: reredos for Church in Philadelphia. "The Last Supper." Executed chiefly in Venice and Murano Smalti.
(*A temporary loan, removed Nov. 2nd.*)

J. W. ODDIE.
268. Wall sconce or brass plaque in ebonized frame: "William Shakespeare."
Designed by J. W. ODDIE.
Executed by J. C. MARTEN.

JAMES POWELL AND SONS.
269. "St. Gabriel": opus sectile and mosaic.
Designed by J. W. BROWN.
Executed by MISS FANNY HARRISON and FREDERICK DUFFIELD.

TOYNBEE HALL SCHOOL AND GUILD OF HANDICRAFT.

270. Copper repoussé work : three 15 in. plates, one pan, one bowl, one 9 in. plate.

Designed by JOHN PEARSON.
Executed by THE GUILD.

THOS. GODFREY AND SONS.

271. Dish, in Old German style, representing boar hunt in centre: wrought copper.

J. W. ODDIE.

272. Brass sconce: "Fox, Bishop of Winchester, founder of C.C.C., Oxford.

Designed by J. W. ODDIE.
Executed by J. C. MARTEN.

F. W. POMEROY.

273. Statuette in bronzed plaster: " In Arcady."

CLEMENT HEATON.

274. Pair of copper vases, decorated with Cloisonné mosaic.

MRS. ERNEST HART.

275. Pair of "O'Neill" curtains: in indigo and Indian red. Embroidered with flax on flax.

MRS. E. HART—*continued.*
Designed by MISS AIMÉE CAR-
PENTER.
Executed by AN IRISH VILLAGE
CLASS.
275 a. Embroidered screen.
Designed and executed by MISS
PARKER.

MRS. AND JANE A. MORRIS.
276. Portière : worked with silks
on linen.
Designed by WILLIAM MORRIS.
Executed by MRS. WILLIAM
MORRIS and JANE A. MORRIS.

MARY SARGANT.
276 a. Study of a lion.

TOYNBEE HALL SCHOOL AND GUILD OF HANDICRAFT.
277. Plate in brass, repoussé.
Designed by JOHN PEARSON.
Executed by THE GUILD.

JAMES POWELL AND SONS.
278. Seven pieces of glass and
hammered iron.
Designed by HARRY JAMES
POWELL.

G

CENTURY GUILD OF ARTISTS.

279. Balcony: Panels.
Designed by A. MACKMURDO.
Modelled by KELLOCK BROWN.
Cast by HANDYSIDE AND Co.

DECORATIVE NEEDLEWORK SOCIETY.

279 a. Couvrette embroidered in crewels.
Designed by MARY GEMMELL.

MISS BURDEN.

280. Embroidery in worsted and silk. " Penelope."

281. Embroidery in worsted and silk. " Hippolyte."

282. Embroidery in worsted and silk. " Helen of Troy."

W. A. S. BENSON.

283. Brass and copper fountain.
Designed by W. A. S. BENSON.
Executed by J. LOVEGROVE.

MARY SARGANT.

284. Decorative Panel. " June."

J. CONRAD DRESSLER.

285. Terra cotta bust.

SOMERS CLARKE AND J. T. MICKLETHWAITE.

286 & 287. Drawing of pulpit in St. Martin's Church, Brighton, with first model of one of the sides.

Designed by SOMERS CLARKE.

Executed by J. E. KNOX.

J. ALDAM HEATON.

288. Stained glass window.

Designed and drawn by E. I. TAYLOR.

Colours arranged, leading, etc., by J. ALDAM HEATON.

Executed by J. ALDAM HEATON.

ROBINSON AND ROBSON.

289. A pair of wrought iron Carriage gates: hammered work.

Designed by ROBINSON AND ROBSON, and executed by them, with the assistance of the late BENJAMIN BRIGGS as smith, and J. UNDERHILL as fitter.

J. ERSKINE KNOX.

290. Font cover: in oak: style of fifteenth century (late).

Designed by SOMERS CLARKE.

Carved by J. ERSKINE KNOX.

The joiners' work executed by DAVID TROUGHTON.

T. R. SPENCE.

291. Design for wall decoration : stencilled in oil-colours.

291 a. Oak cabinet.
Designed by T. R. SPENCE.
Executed by R. HEDLEY.

291 b. Table lamp in Copper. Wrought, turned, and embossed.

291 c. Lock and finger plate in polished brass, with applied shields and drop handle.

291 d. Finger plates in embossed copper.

291 e. Bell pull and chain, in wrought iron with panelled centres.

291 f. Drawer and cupboard handles in wrought copper.

291 c. to 291 f. all { Designed by T. R. SPENCE.
Executed by ALFRED SHIRLEY.

RHODA AND AGNES GARRETT.

292. Wood panelling : cupboard, etc.

Designed by RHODA and AGNES GARRETT.

Panel paper cut and printed by WM. WOOLLAMS AND CO.

R. AND A. GARRETT—*continued.*
Carpet : handmade.
Designed by RHODA and AGNES
GARRETT.
Executed by GATES AND MAR-
SHALL.

Furniture : comprising long chair,
tea table, fire-side chair, and flower
stand.
Designed by RHODA and AGNES
GARRETT.
Executed by W. A. AND S. SMEE.

Pendant and candle sconce : in
brass and copper : hammered and
pierced.
Designed by AGNES GARRETT
and ALFRED SHIRLEY.
Executed by ALFRED SHIRLEY.

HERBERT A. BONE.
293. Cartoon for tapestry: "King
Alfred in the Danish camp." Water-
colour, designed in reverse, for reproduction in a low-warp loom.
The labels on the border engrossed
by S. SOUTHALL BONE.

ROYAL TAPESTRY WORKS,
WINDSOR.
293 a. Tapestry: " King Alfred in

the Danish camp." Woven by hand on a warp in wool.

Designed by HERBERT A. BONE.

Executed by GEORGE ELEMAN, WILLIAM HAINES, JEAN FOUSSA-DIER.

WALTER CRANE.

294. Dish : in copper repoussé.

295. Sconce : in brass repoussé.

THOS. GODFREY AND SONS.

296. Octagonal sconce in Old English style, with candle tray supported by swans : wrought and chased brass.

CENTURY GUILD OF ARTISTS.

297. Bracket figure : design for architectural decoration : in plaster, for stone or terra cotta.

Designed and executed by B. CRESWICK.

ELGOOD BROS.

298. Finger plate : in bronze repoussé: design adapted from Japanese flower.

ELGOOD BROS.—*continued.*

299. Lock and finger-plate : in brass repoussé : Artichokes treated conventionally.

THOS. GODFREY AND SONS.

300. Wall light in Queen Anne style : in wrought and chased brass, mounted on black wood.　　　·

300 a. Octagonal mirror frame in Old English style : wrought in brass and mounted on oak backboard.

J. STARKIE GARDNER AND CO.

301 & 318. Iron grills.
Executed by A. W. ELLWOOD, JUN.

MRS. ERNEST HART.

302. Bed coverlet. "Hamilton."

L. A. SHUFFREY.

303. Chimney piece : in painted pine.
Designed by L. A. SHUFFREY.
Tiles designed by CHAS. JOHNSON.
Executed by JAS. HUTCHINSON (foreman).

HENRI J. L. J. MASSÉ.

303 a.   Footman: in brass: pierced and chased work.

Date of design about 1700.

Executed by H. J. L. J. MASSÉ.

LONGDEN AND CO.

304.   Mantelpiece and grate.

Designed by JOHN F. BENTLEY.

Executed by LONGDEN AND CO., assisted by F. STRIDE, J. DYSON, and B. COLDWELL.

305.   Grate.

Designed by J. F. BENTLEY.

Executed by LONGDEN AND CO., assisted by B. COLDWELL.

306.   Fender.

Designed by J. F. BENTLEY.

Executed by LONGDEN AND CO., assisted by W. KNOWLES.

307.   Wrought-iron bracket for gas.

Designed by J. D. SEDDING.

Executed by LONGDEN AND CO., assisted by J. CLUCAS.

308.   Wrought-iron bracket for lamps.

Designed by J. D. SEDDING.

Executed by LONGDEN AND CO., assisted by J. CLUCAS.

LONGDEN AND CO.—*continued.*

309. Portion of wrought-iron and copper railing.
Designed by G. C. HORSLEY.
Executed by LONGDEN AND CO., assisted by J. CLUCAS and W. BULLAS.

310. Brass cross.
Designed by J. D. SEDDING.
Executed by LONGDEN AND CO., assisted by J. MARSHALL and J. B. COLDWELL.

311. Brass Altar candlesticks.
Designed by J. D. SEDDING.
Executed by LONGDEN AND CO., assisted by N. BULLAS.

312. Wrought-iron fire-irons.
Designed by H. LONGDEN.
Executed by LONGDEN AND CO., assisted by J. CLUCAS and IBRAHIM of Gujerat.

313. Wrought-iron grate.
Designed by H. LONGDEN (in W. De Morgan's Exhibit, No. 53).
Executed by LONGDEN AND CO., assisted by B. COLDWELL.

314. Polished iron grate.
Designed by H. LONGDEN.
Executed by LONGDEN AND CO., assisted by J. CLUCAS and J. DUTTON.

CENTURY GUILD OF ARTISTS.

315. Bracket figure in plaster (for bronze): Subject, "Miner at work."

Designed and executed by B. CRESWICK.

J. STARKIE GARDNER AND CO.

316. Lamp bracket: in wrought-iron.

Executed by J. CASLAKE.

317. Candle branch: in wrought-iron.

Executed by J. CASLAKE.

318. Grill: in wrought-iron.

THOMAS GODFREY AND CO.

319. Oval sconce in the Flemish style: in repoussé and chased brass.

TOYNBEE HALL SCHOOL AND GUILD OF HANDICRAFT.

320. Plate in copper, repoussé. Designed by JOHN WILLIAMS. Executed by THE GUILD.

TOYNBEE HALL—*continued.*

321. Plate in German silver, repoussé.

Designed by JOHN PEARSON.
Executed by THE GUILD.

J. W. ODDIE.

322. Brass plaque and copper tray : repoussé.

Designed by J. W. ODDIE.
Executed by J. C. MARTEN.

J. STEBBINGS.

323. Specimens of repoussé work in iron and brass.

SIDNEY A. AUSTIN.

324. Metal panel : chased and repoussé.

FRANCIS SCAIFE.

325. Door-plate : in brass and iron.

F. W. POMEROY.

326. Statuette in bronzed plaster : "Giotto."

THOS. GODFREY AND SONS.

327. Five finger plates, two door knobs and two escutcheons, two bell

T. GODFREY AND SONS—*continued.*
levers, two copper trays, two brass
trays, one flat candle : wrought in
brass, copper, and nickel, and chased.

Vesper lamp and bracket in Venetian style : in wrought and chased
brass, mounted on plush.

Pair of oval wall lights in Louis
XV. style : in brass, beaten and
chased.

Mirror frame in Louis XV. style :
mounted on plush, in repoussé and
chased brass.

TOYNBEE HALL SCHOOL AND GUILD OF HANDICRAFT.

328.　Copper plaque : repoussé.

328a.　Copper bowl : repoussé.

J. W. ODDIE.

329.　Sconce : in brass, repoussé.
Designed by J. W. ODDIE.
Executed by J. C. MARTEN.

TOYNBEE HALL SCHOOL AND GUILD OF HANDICRAFT.

330.　Copper plaque : repoussé.

THOS. GODFREY AND SONS.
331. Alms-dish in Old English style : wrought copper.

TOYNBEE HALL SCHOOL AND GUILD OF HANDICRAFT.
332. Copper plaque : repoussé.

GEORGE SIMONDS.
333. Silver loving-cup : partly cast.

EDWIN GEO. HARDY.
334. Hanging lamp : in brass. Designed by EDWIN GEO. HARDY. Executed by T. BISHOP.

MRS. ERNEST HART.
335. " O'Neill " Curtain. Executed by EMPLOYÉS OF THE DONEGAL INDUSTRIAL FUND.

HEATON'S MOSAIC L^D.
336. Cloisonné-mosaic decoration as applied to pillars. Designed by CLEMENT HEATON.

CENTURY GUILD OF ARTISTS.

336 a. Study for gargoyle : cast in plaster, for stone or terra cotta.

Designed and executed by B. CRESWICK.

WALTER CRANE.

337. Gas lamp : in repoussé brass and copper.

Designed by WALTER CRANE.

Executed by WALTER CRANE and JERRY BARRETT.

W. A. S. BENSON.

338. Lamp in copper and brass.
Designed by W. A. S. BENSON.
Executed by J. LOVEGROVE.

J. STARKIE GARDNER AND CO.

339. Lamp : in wrought iron.
Executed by J. IMSON.

340. Dog : in wrought iron for grate.

Executed by JAMES WARD.

341. Lamp : in wrought iron.
Executed by THOMAS KENDALL.

MINTON AND CO.

342 to 350. ⎫
351 to 361. ⎬ Three Cases of Pottery.
362 to 380. ⎭

342. Tray in Parian : " Pâte sur pâte."
Decorated by ALBOIN BIRKS.

343. Two china vases.
DESIRÉ LEROY, artist.
ALBERT DUDLEY, potter.

344. Two vases.
Painted by R. PILSBURY.

345. Two pierced china vases.
JESSIE POPE, potter.

346. Vases : " Pâte sur pâte."
Decorated by ARTHUR MORGAN.

347. Two Parian vases : " decorated " Pâte sur pâte."

348. Dessert plates.
Decorated by LAWRENCE BIRKS.

349. Two china vases.
Painted by DESIRÉ LEROY.

350. Two Parian vases.
Decorated by ALBOIN BIRKS.

351. Dessert plate : china painted on soft glaze.
A. BOULLEMIER, painter.
F. MART, gilder.

MINTON AND CO.—*continued.*

352 & 353. Two pairs of china vases.
Painted by R. PILSBURY.

354. Dessert plate.
Painted by AARON GREEN.

355. Vase with cover.
A. BOULLEMIER, artist.
JOHN HARRISON, potter.

356. China vase.
A. BOULLEMIER, artist.
ALBERT DUDLEY, potter.

357. Two candelabra.
ALBERT DUDLEY, potter.

358. Parian ewer.
J. POPE, potter.

359. China dinner plate.
Designed by LEON ARNOUX.
Gilt by JOHN MARROW.

360. Two jardinières.
ALBERT WRIGHT, artist.
JESSIE POPE, potter.

361. China tray.
A. BOULLEMIER, painter.
THOMAS GRIFFITHS, potter.

362. Two Parian vases.
Decorated by THOMAS TAYLOR.

363. Pair of china vases.
RICHARD PILSBURY, painter.

MINTON AND CO.—*continued.*
364.   Pair of Parian vases.
ALBERT WRIGHT, painter.
PETER STOTT, gilder.

365.   Pair of earthenware vases.
Painted under glaze by W. MUSSILL.

366.   "Amazon."
Executed by HENRY ASTON.

367.   Pair of earthenware plaques.
Painted by WILLIAM PILSBURY.

368.   Pair of earthenware slabs.
By L. M. SOLON.

369.   Earthenware plaque.
Painted by W. MUSSILL.

370.   Pair of earthenware plaques.
Painted by W. MUSSILL.

MAW AND CO.
381.   (a) Specimens of tiles.
Designed by LEWIS F. DAY.
Executed by MAW AND CO.

(b) Specimens of tiles.
Designed by A. C. WEATHERSTON.
Executed by MAW AND CO.

(c) Specimens of tiles.
Designed by C. JOHNSON.
Executed by MAW AND CO.

MAW AND CO.—*continued.*

(d)   Specimens of tiles.
   Designed by J. BRADBURN.
   Executed by MAW AND CO.

(e)   Specimens of tiles.
   Designed by J. BRADBURN and W.
MOORE.
   Executed by MAW AND CO.

(f)   Specimens of tiles.
   Designed by — ROWORTH.
   Executed by MAW AND CO.

(g)   Specimens of tiles.
   Designed by WALTER CRANE.
   Painted by W. MOORE.

(h)   Specimens of tiles.
   Designed and painted by C. H.
TEMPLE.

(i)   Specimens of tiles.
   Painted by C. H. TEMPLE.

(k)   Specimens of tiles.
   Painted by A. CHILDE.

(l)   Specimens of tiles.
   Painted by W. EVANS.

(m)   Specimens of tiles.
   Designed by W. LODGE.
   Painted by C. H. TEMPLE.

MAW AND CO.—*continued.*
382. Stand of lustre pottery.

Objects marked "A" designed by
LEWIS F. DAY.
Objects marked "B" designed by
C. JOHNSON.
Executed by MAW AND CO.

VERITY BROTHERS.
383. Electrolier: in handwrought
polished brass.
Designed by G. F. HENNEY.
Executed by T. FAWKES, J. D.
WILLIAMS, J. R. WILCOXSON.

(The following are in Case A.)

HARRY J. SALTER.
385. Candlestick: in wrought iron.

JAMES POWELL AND SONS.
386. Thirteen pieces English
Soda-lime glass.
Designed by HARRY JAMES
POWELL.

HUNT AND ROSKELL. (By kind permission of W. M. Cazalet, Esq.)

387. Waist belt and watch pocket of wrought gold, illustrating "The Story of the Year," which is represented by panels containing subjects characteristic of the various months and seasons. Each panel is divided by flowers typical of the months.

Designed and executed by GEORGE CARTER.

387 a. Blotting-book cover: in repoussé and pierced silver.

Designed and executed by GEORGE DEERE.

J. STARKIE GARDNER & CO.
388. Candle-stand in wrought iron.
Executed by FRANK BIRKETT.

W. J. DEERE.
389. Specimen of line engraving.

W. REYNOLDS-STEPHENS.
390. A dance name and number holder.

(The above are in Case A.)

MRS. ERNEST HART.

391. Alb of Limerick lace: in linen thread on net by a tambour needle.

Designed by the NUNS OF KENMARE.

Executed by a LIMERICK LACE WORKER, employed by the DONEGAL INDUSTRIAL FUND.

391 a. Case of wools.

Dyed by EMPLOYÉS OF THE DONEGAL INDUSTRIAL FUND.

A. J. SMITH.

392. Frieze in plaster.

CHARLOTTE H. SPIERS.

393. Frieze in oil: painted with tulips.

JOHN WILSON.

394. Model in clay (for terra cotta) of vase: unfinished.

HEATON'S MOSAIC L.

395. Plaster decoration for a frieze.

396 & 397. Cloisonné-mosaic decoration for friezes.

JAMES ELLIOTT.

398. Wall hanging or portière : painted in lustra, outlined with work.

Designed by JAMES ELLIOTT.

Executed by MISS FLEMING and MISS ELLIOTT.

WILLIAM MORRIS.

399. "Holland Park" carpet : handmade.

Designed by WILLIAM MORRIS.

Executed by MORRIS AND CO.

JAMES ELLIOTT.

400. Portière : painted in lustra on Roman satin, outlined with work.

Designed by JAMES ELLIOTT.

Executed by MISS FLEMING.

GALLERY.

CAMPBELL SMITH AND CO.

401. Six designs of figures for Council Chamber, Guildhall.
Designed by F. G. SMITH.

CENTURY GUILD OF ARTISTS.

401 a. Tail-pieces by SELWYN IMAGE.
Cut by C. PADDY.

CAMPBELL SMITH AND CO.

402. Three designs.
(1) King Alfred and the Arctic Voyagers.
(2) Admiral Howard attacking the Armada.
(3) Peter the Great visiting the Dockyard at Deptford.
Designed by F. G. SMITH.

T. M. ROOKE.

403. Book decoration : specimen of proposed decoration for a history of the Siege of Troy.

F. HAMILTON JACKSON.

404. Sketch for decoration: side of a hall: in water colour.

CENTURY GUILD OF ARTISTS.

404 a.   Initial letters and tail-pieces by H. P. HORNE.
Printed by the CHISWICK PRESS.

404 b. Music, drawn by H. P. HORNE, and printed by the CHISWICK PRESS for the Century Guild "Hobby Horse."

HENRY HOLIDAY.

405. Designs for memorial windows in the Presbyterian Church, Forfar.

GAETANO MEO.

406. Panel (in chalk) for stained glass : " Fox-glove."

HENRY HOLIDAY.

407. Nude studies for mosaic, representing " The Last Supper."

HENRY HOLIDAY—*continued.*

408. Pencil sketch for stained glass window for a church in New York.

409. Nude studies for "Lazarus": stained glass.

LEWIS F. DAY.
410. Twelve designs for surface decoration : reduced from wall papers, cretonnes, etc.

ARTHUR LEVERETT.
411. Frame of *Proof* wood-engravings.
Designed by WALTER CRANE.
Executed by ARTHUR LEVERETT.

LEWIS F. DAY.
412. Book decoration : initial letters, etc. Printed from wood or process blocks.
Designed by LEWIS F. DAY.
Wood engravings executed by W. H. HOOPER.

413. Book decoration : two designs for book covers, three periodical covers, one heading.

H

REGINALD HALLWARD.

414. Water-colour drawing: design for book-cover: "Flowers of Paradise."

Water-colour drawing: illustration for "Flowers of Paradise."

Designs for needlework: in water-colour.

MRS. REGINALD HALLWARD.

415. Design for book-cover: in line and tint.

WALTER CRANE.

416. Eight of the original drawings made for "The First of May": in lead pencil on thick Whatman's paper.

417. The set of original drawings for "The Sirens Three": in pen and Indian ink on card.

418. Original designs for book-headings: (two frames). On card, in pen and Indian ink.

419 & 420. Original designs to illustrate Grimm's Household Stories: (three frames). On card, in pen and ink. Some of the full pages are done with a fine brush and lamp-black.

G. P. JACOMB HOOD.

421 & 423. Designs and reproductions of design for "Aucassin and Nicolette."
Reproduced in facsimile by THE TYPOGRAPHIC ETCHING CO.

422. Reproductions of designs for " The Happy Prince," by Oscar Wilde.
Reproduced in facsimile by THE TYPOGRAPHIC ETCHING CO.

HEYWOOD SUMNER.

424. Headings for English Illustrated Magazine: in black and white.

425. Illustrations and proofs for "The Besom Maker": in black and white.

426. Illustrations for "Undine": in black and white.

HENRY HOLIDAY.

427. Wood engravings: not facsimile, copied from water-colour monochromes.
Executed by W. BABBAGE.

T. ERAT HARRISON.

428. Book decorations: two bookplates: one reproduction of bookplate: two illustrations.

GEORGE PORTER.

429. Initial letters, headings and caricatures (*Proofs*).

EDMUND EVANS.

430. Specimen of colour printing from engraved wooden blocks.
Designed by WALTER CRANE.
Executed by EDMUND EVANS.
Sheets showing stages of the process of colour printing from blocks.

J. HUNGERFORD POLLEN.

431. Sketch of wall painting : "The Romans in England."

432. Design of plaster and timber ceiling, Blickling Hall.

433. Fire-place : St. George's Hall : water-colour.

434. Sketch of large wall painting at Alton Towers : "Henry V. before Harfleur."

435. Design for plaster ceiling : "The Seasons."

436. Sketch of part of decorations : Ingestre Hall : water-colour.

WILLIAM HENRY JEWITT.

437. Study in Renaissance decoration.

C. F. A. VOYSEY.
438. Photograph of memorial to Carlyle.
Designed by C. F. A. VOYSEY.
Executed by B. CRESWICK.

HARRY ARNOLD.
439. Three Chapters of Love.

AUDLEY MACKWORTH.
440. Design for wall painting.

MATTHEW W. WEBB.
441. Water-colour painting: single figure.

B. AND F. GAST.
442. A decoration.

W. R. LETHABY.
443. Design for a room: in black and pearl.
444. Design for decoration of a room: in panelling and paint.

J. R. SPENCE.
445. Decorative figure: "Persephone."

MRS. RUSSELL BARRINGTON.
446. Oil painting: "Girl Singing."

F. HAMILTON JACKSON.

447. "S. Perpetua": decorative figure: oil colour on gold ground with raised pattern.

T. M. ROOKE.

448. Needle and appliqué work. Story of the Argo. (The Golden Fleece.)
Designed by T. M. ROOKE.
Executed by E. L. JONES.

449. Needle and appliqué work. Story of the Argo. (Medea and Circe.)
Designed by T. M. ROOKE.
Executed by E. L. JONES.

450. Needle and appliqué work. Story of the Argo. (Pelias dead, and festivity on the Argo's return.)
Designed by T. M. ROOKE.
Executed by E. L. JONES.

GEORGE PORTER.

451. An Angel.

MORRIS AND CO.

452. Cretonne hanging.
Designed by WILLIAM MORRIS

453. Carved wood seat.

TOYNBEE HALL SCHOOL AND GUILD OF HANDICRAFT.

454. Specimen of painting in enamel.

W. A. S. BENSON.

454a. Lamp in brass, with onyx panels.
Designed by W. A. S. BENSON.
Executed by J. LOVEGROVE.

TOYNBEE HALL SCHOOL AND GUILD OF HANDICRAFT.

455. Dish: in copper repoussé work.

CHARLOTTE H. SPIERS.

456. Plaque: painted with white lilies.

A. G. COOPER.

457 & 458. Brass plaques: repoussé work.

J. W. ODDIE.

459. Brass tray, vesica-shaped.
Designed by J. W. ODDIE.
Executed by J. C. MARTEN.

A. G. COOPER.

460.   Pewter tray.

DONEGAL NEEDLEWORK SOCIETY.

460 a. Bed-cover.

TOYNBEE HALL SCHOOL AND GUILD OF HANDICRAFT.

461.   Frame in copper : repoussé work.

CHISWICK PRESS.

(CHARLES WHITTINGHAM AND CO.)

Printed Books.

462 a.   The Book of Common Prayer, etc., folio, 1843. In black letter, printed in red and black.   One of the set of 7 vols. of Books of Common Prayer.

462 b. Breviarium Aberdonense : 2 vols. 4to. 1854.   Printed in red and black.

462 c.   The New Testament : translated by John Wycliffe, circa 1380 : in black letter.   4to. 1848.

462 d.   Altar Service Book : folio, London, 1867.   In red and black.

462 e.   The Book of Common Prayer : 8vo. 1864.   In red and black.

CHISWICK PRESS—*continued.*
Border to every page copied from
Geoffrey Tory's Missale.

462 f.   Lady Willoughby's Diary.
Cr. 8vo. 1845.   This book was the
first in the production of which Caslon's "old style" type was revived by
the Chiswick Press.

462 g.   The Book of Common
Prayer: 8vo. 1853.   A reprint of the
Book known as Queen Elizabeth's
Prayer Book, from the portrait of that
queen being on the back of the title-
pages.   The border to every page,
with the Dance of Death, is exactly
reproduced.

462 h.   Order of the Administration
of Holy Communion: 4to. 1848.

462 i.   The Book of Common Prayer,
Noted: By John Merbecke, 1550.
Printed in red and black : the music-
stave red, notation black.   1844.

462 k.   Homer's Iliad and Odyssey,
2 vols.   Diamond Classics, 64mo.
M.D.CCCXXXI.

462 l.   The Life of Mrs. Godolphin.
1888.   Caslon type on Van Gelder
paper, with rule borders.

H 2

CHISWICK PRESS—*continued.*

462 m.   Johann Schöner von Karl-
stadt.   1888.   A specimen of the
special Chiswick Press fount.

463.   Thomas Gray's Poems and
Letters.   4to.   1879.   This is the pre-
sentation "leaving book," printed for
DR. HORNBY, Eton College.

463 a.   John Milton : Paradise Lost.
4to. 1873.   Facsimile reproduction of
first edition of 1667.

463 b.   Catalogue of Basil Montagu
Pickering's Books : Crown 8vo.   In-
cluding the Publications of the late
William Pickering.   Printed in imitation of an Aldine volume and exhibit-
ing a cheap form of catalogue printing.

463 c.   Who Spoils Our New English Books.   1884.   A quaint brochure
by the late HENRY STEVENS of Ver-
mont.

The books here exhibited were
printed between the years 1831 and
1888, under several practical manage-
ments, commencing with the first
CHARLES WHITTINGHAM down to the
present manager, CHARLES THOMAS
JACOBI.

CENTURY GUILD OF ARTISTS.

463 d. " The Century Guild Hobby Horse."

Printed at the CHISWICK PRESS: ornaments designed by HERBERT P. HORNE.

R. AND R. CLARK.

463 e. Printed book : Grimm's Household Stories, with pictures designed by WALTER CRANE, and engraved by JOSEPH SWAIN.

HEATON'S MOSAIC L.

464. Brass plaque repoussé: the brass embossed by a new process invented by CLEMENT HEATON.

Designed by CLEMENT HEATON.

Executed by WM. J. YATES and CLEMENT HEATON.

J. W. ODDIE.

465. Copper tray : repoussé work.

Designed by J. W. ODDIE.

Executed by J. C. MARTEN.

MORRIS AND CO.

465 a. Three "Hammersmith" carpets.

DECORATIVE NEEDLEWORK SOCIETY.
465 b. Altar frontal embroidered in silk and gold.

Designed by MARY GEMMELL.

ELGOOD BROTHERS.
466. Alms-dish in brass : repoussé work.

EDWARD HAMMOND.
467. Stained glass window : " St. George."

F. HAMILTON JACKSON.
468. Stained glass window : Painted on glass.

Executed by F. HAMILTON JACKSON and B. ANDREW LILLIE.

CHRISTOPHER W. WHALL.
469. Three panels of lead-tracery : domestic window.

LEWIS F. DAY.
470. Two stained glass shutter panels.

CAMPBELL SMITH AND CO.

471. Glass panel: "The Cock and Jewel."
Designed by F. G. SMITH.
Executed by CAMPBELL SMITH AND CO.

472. Glass panel.
Designed by F. G. SMITH.
Executed by CAMPBELL SMITH AND CO.

473. Glass panel.
Designed by J. D. WATSON.
Executed by CAMPBELL SMITH AND CO.

474. Glass panel: "Peter the Great at the Dockyard." [*Vide* No. 402.]

475. Six stained glass panels. Subject, "Orpheus."
Designed by F. G. SMITH.

H. ARTHUR KENNEDY.

476. Painted glass: female figure holding medallion of Homer, with frieze subject from the Iliad.

Painted glass: female figure holding medallion of Dante, with frieze subject from the Purgatorio.

H. A. KENNEDY—*continued.*
Painted glass: " Knight and Water-maiden."

Painted glass: "Mercutio."

Painted glass : " A Nightmare."

HENRY HOLIDAY.
477. Stained glass window :
"Music."
Designed by HENRY HOLLIDAY.
Painted by WILLIAM GLASBY, J.
E. PENWARDEN, ALBERT LAWREN-
SON; in the employ of JAMES POWELL
AND SONS.

JOHN AND WILLIAM GUTHRIE.
478. Domestic glass.

E. BURNE-JONES.
479. Four lights in stained glass.
Subjects from the San Grail.
Designed by E. BURNE-JONES.
Executed by MORRIS AND CO.

AGNES L. HINE.
480. Gipsy table: in carved wood.

W. AUMONIER.
481. Oak panel: example of
Gothic treatment of carving.

JOSEPH PHILLIPS.
482. Portion of a carved frieze.

E. M. MOORE.
483. Carved frieze for a music-room.

HOME ARTS AND INDUS-TRIES ASSOCIATION.
483 a. Bench in carved oak.

W. AUMONIER.
484. Mirror frame: oak and mahogany, carved and inlaid.

485. Oak carving : pilaster in the style of the Italian Renaissance.

H. CASTLE AND SONS.
486. Oak carving: miniature replicas of "Atlas," after the two stern figures taken off the "Téméraire" when broken up in 1838.
Designed by SIDNEY N. CASTLE.
Executed by J. E. HELLYER.

R. W. REDHEAD.
487. Spinning stool. Design adapted from old stool.

MRS. R. BATEMAN.
488. Bowl in light wood : black and incised design.

THOS. GODFREY AND SONS.

489. Pair of oval sconces: in brass repoussé work.

JAMES OSMOND.

490. Carved oak panel.

FRANCES EDITH PACE.

491. Frieze in Italian walnut.

HOME ARTS AND INDUS-TRIES ASSOCIATION.

492. Oak table.
Executed by DAVID DRURY, JOHN HIGGINS, — SHARMAN.

JOHN J. SHAW.

492 a. Decoration of a drawing-room.

ADA M. EVANS.

493. Specimens of brass repoussé work.

AGNES BOYD.

494. Candlestick: with old Danish ornament.

494a. Crumb-scoop: in chased copper.

A. G. COOPER.

494b. Three specimens of chased and repoussé work in pewter.

TOYNBEE HALL SCHOOL AND GUILD OF HANDICRAFT.

494c. Copper plaque: repoussé work.

H. B. BARE.

495. Inglenook for Aymestry Court.

PHILIP NEWMAN.

496. Designs for stained glass windows.

B. AND F. GAST.

497. Design for Mantelpiece.

H. W. LONSDALE.

498. Designs for wall-paintings, at Mount Stuart House, Rothesay.

H. B. BARE.

499. Decoration for a dining-room.

PHILIP NEWMAN.

500. Design for stained glass window.

CARL SCHNEIDER.

501. Specimens of engraving.

W. S. COLEMAN.

502. Designs (to be enlarged) for decorative panels.

T. ERAT HARRISON.

503. Panel in oil on silver ground: "Water."

504. Panel in oil: "Night."

505. Panel in oil on gold and silver ground: "Fire."

J. ALDAM HEATON.

506. Decorative panel: "Hibernia."

MARY SARGANT.

507. Studies of flowers.

508, 508a, 508b. Designs for frieze.

R. PILSBURY.

509. Study of an orchid.

511. Study of chrysanthemums.

MRS. A. PRADEAU.

510. Panel: "Evening Primroses."

A. B. DONALDSON.

512. Design for a mosaic Cross.

J. HUNGERFORD POLLEN.
513. Wall painting : part of the decoration of Crabbet House.

JOHN EYRE.
513 a. Piano front : subject, " Vocal and Instrumental Music."

F. VINCENT HART.
514. Cartoon for stained glass for library window : " The Dawn of History."

CHRISTOPHER W. WHALL.
515. Design in ornamental lead-tracery for domestic window.

A. B. DONALDSON.
516. Design for a plaque : " Benedicite omnia opera."

JOHN STAINES BABB.
517. Decorative design : "Hadrian."

INDEX OF
EXHIBITORS, ARTISTS, AND CRAFTSMEN.

INDEX OF
EXHIBITORS, ARTISTS, AND CRAFTSMEN.

The addresses of Exhibitors only are given.

The figures at the end refer to the corresponding numbers in the Catalogue.

ETCHING, THE TYPOGRAPHIC, CO., 3, Ludgate Circus Buildings, E.C.   421-423.
EVANS, ADA M., Witley, Surrey.   493.
EVANS, EDMUND, Racquet Court, Fleet Street, E.C.   430.
EVANS, W.   381l.
EYRE, JOHN.   513a.

FAULKNER, KATE,   35,   Queen Square, Bloomsbury, W.C.   266a.
FAWKES, T.   383.
FLAVETT, WILLIAM.   52b.
FLEMING, MISS.   398, 400.
FOUSSADIER, JEAN, Royal Tapestry Works, Windsor.   293a.
FOX, G. E.   80, 81.

GARDNER, J. STARKIE, AND CO., 29, Albert Embankment, S.E.   301, 316-318, 339-341, 388.
GARRARD, F., Westferry Road, Millwall, E.   38, 51.
GARRETT, RHODA AND AGNES, 2, Gower Street, W.C.   292.
GAST, B. F., 12, Noel Street, Islington, N   56, 442, 497.
GATES AND MARSHALL.   292.
GELL, MRS. NEWMAN, 52, Old Stein, Brighton.   254.
GEMMELL, MARY.   143b, 279a, 465b.
GILLAM, W.   266a.
GLASBY, WILLIAM.   477.
GODFREY, THOMAS, 27, Chatham Road, Wandsworth Common, S.W.   68, 76.
GODFREY, THOMAS, AND SONS, 27, Chatham Road, Wandsworth Common, S.W.   271, 296, 300, 300a, 319, 327, 331, 489.
GREEN, AARON.   354.

GREEN, AVELING, 2, Steele's Studios, Havre-
stock Hill, N.W. 214, 215, 218.
GRIFFITHS, THOMAS. 361.
GUTHRIE, JOHN AND WILLIAM, 231, Oxford
Street, W. 478.
GWYNN, J. 144.

HAINES, WILLIAM, Royal Tapestry Works,
Windsor. 293a.
HAITÉ, GEORGE C., Ormsby Lodge, The
Avenue, Bedford Park, W. 60, 90, 91, 95.
HALLWARD, REGINALD, 3, Brook Green, W.
414.
HALLWARD, MRS., 3, Brook Green, W. 415.
HAMMOND, EDWARD, 207, Brecknock Road
N. 467.
HANDICRAFT, TOYNBEE HALL SCHOOL AND
GUILD OF, Toynbee Hall, Commercial
Street, Whitechapel, E. 270, 277, 320, 321,
328, 328a, 330, 332, 454, 455, 461, 494c.
HANDYSIDE AND CO. 279.
HARDY, EDWIN GEORGE, 17, Brunswick
Gardens, W. 334.
HARRISON, FANNY. 269.
HARRISON, JOHN. 355.
HARRISON, T. ERAT, 3, Bath Road, Bedford
Park, Chiswick, W. 428, 503-505.
HART, MRS. ERNEST, 43, Wigmore Street,
W. 21a, 36a, 103a, 275, 275a, 302, 335,
391.
HART, F. VINCENT, 50, Oxford and Cam-
bridge Mansions, N.W. 514.
HARVEY, FREDERICK. 105, 106, 108.
HAY, THOMAS WALLACE, 21, St. Mary's
Terrace, Paddington, W. 234.
HEATON, MRS. ALDAM, 27, Charlotte Street,
Bedford Square, W.C. 11, 16.

IBRAHIM. 312.
IMAGE, SELWYN. 139, 170a, 170b, 401a.
IMSON, J. 339.
IONIDES, A. 266a.
IRISH GIRLS, A CLASS OF. 36a.
IRISH VILLAGE CLASS. 275a.

JACK, G. 50, 50g.
JACKSON, F. HAMILTON, 35, Woodstock
Road, Bedford Park, W. 205, 404, 447,
468.
JACOBI, C. T. 462, 463.
JEFFREY AND CO., 64, Essex Road, Isling-
ton, N. 61-83, 88, 126.
JEWITT, WILLIAM HENRY, 4, Torriano
Cottages, Camden Road, N.W. 437.
JOHNSON, C. 303, 381c, 382.
JONES, E. L. 448-450.

KEIDEL, A., 45, Gerrard Street, Colebrook
Row, Islington, N. 232, 233.
KENDALL, THOMAS. 341.
KENMARE, NUNS OF. 391.
KENNEDY, H. ARTHUR, 27, Endsleigh Gar-
dens, N.W. 476.
KNIGHT, CHARLES. 50c, 50h.
KNOWLES, W. 306.
KNOX, J. E. 286, 287, 290.

LATTIMER, JAMES, School of Art, Cavendish
Street, Manchester. 93.
LAWRENSON, ALBERT. 477.
LEEK EMBROIDERY SOCIETY. 52a.
LEIGHTON, R. 120.
LEROY, DÉSIRÉ. 343, 349.
LESLIE, HARRY. 219.
LETHABY, W. R., 20, Calthorpe Street, W.C.
443, 444.

SHEPHERD, J.　266a.

SHERWIN, JAMES.　123.

SHIELDS, FREDERICK J., Sierra House, Lodge
　Place, N.W.　169, 189, 205a.

SHIRLEY, A.　291, 292.

SHUFFREY, L. A., 33, Welbeck Street, W.
　303.

SIDWELL, H.　50, 50g.

SILVER, A.　92.

SIMONDS, GEORGE, 152, Buckingham
　Palace Road, S.W.　333.

SLEATH, JOHN.　50c, 50f, 50h.

SMEE, W. A. AND S.　292.

SMITH, A. J., 7, Musgrave Crescent, Moor
　Park Hill, Fulham, S.W.　392.

SMITH, F. G.　401, 402, 471, 472, 475.

SMITH, J. MOYR, Doune Lodge, Oxford
　Road, Putney, S.W.　110.

SMITH, MARY A., 10, Kensington Court Man-
　sions, W.　8.

SOLON, M. L.　368.

SPENCE, T. R., 45, Rathbone Place, W.
　291a, 291c, 445.

SPIERS, CHARLOTTE H., 4, Berners Street,
　W.　57, 393, 456.

STANHOPE, SPENCER, Villa Nuti, Bellos-
　guardo, Florence.　230, 257.

STANLEY, HON. MRS.　144.

STEADMAN, ELLEN.　49.

STEBBINGS, J., 38, Brewer Street, Golden
　Square, W.　323.

STEPHENS, E. H.　19.

STEVENS, HENRY.　463c.

STEVENSON AND CO.　111.

STEWART, DORA, 12, The Terrace, High
　Street, Kensington, W.　9, 14.

STOTT, PETER.　364.

STRAKER AND CO.　111.

POTTERY · GLASS · PAINTING · ARCHITECTURE · SCULPTURE · METAL WORK · DESIGN

THE · ARTS · AND · CRAFTS · EXHIBITION · SOCIETY ·

www.ingramcontent.com/pod-product-compliance
Lightning Source LLC
Chambersburg PA
CBHW031057280326
41928CB00049B/966